"This book is not only an insightful guide to the art of play direction from a faith-based perspective, but also a book about leadership, which is what good direction is really all about. Elvgren's years of practical experience and insight are present on every page. Every faith-based university theater program needs to make this book required reading for their student directors."

—**Frank Mihelich**, Artistic Director, New Threads Theater Company

"Elvgren is a visionary director and a prolific playwright, a man of the theater who is also a man of God. Throughout my creative life, the energy and imagination of his work and ideas have been an ongoing inspiration. This book is a tremendous gift to further generations of theater artists. It is a concrete and specific expression of the breadth of experience and Spirit-fired passion that have fueled Gillette's own theatrical calling and inspired many others in their own."

—**Ron Reed**, founding Artistic Director, Pacific Theater

"This book sheds a new light on directing the play. Gillette Elvgren has delivered a treat for anyone interested in the theater! The generosity of his wisdom, faith, and experience makes the book a remarkable symposium, memoir, and meditation."

—**Robert Smyth**, Producing Artistic Director, Lamb's Players Theater

Directing Theater

Directing Theater

A Christian Perspective

GILLETTE ELVGREN

Integratio Press

Pasco, Washington

DIRECTING THEATER: A Christian Perspective

This is a publication of Trinity House, a Division of Integratio Press.

Integratio Press is an Imprint of the Christianity and Communication Studies Network:
11503 Easton Dr.
Pasco, WA 99301

www.theccsn.com

For questions and feedback, email the author: gillelvjr@gmail.com

Cover design: Carol O'Callaghan
Interior design: Atritex Technologies
Images: Depositphotos

PAPERBACK ISBN: 978-1-959685-07-4
EBOOK ISBN: 978-1-959685-08-1

Library of Congress Control Number: 2023945333

Table of Contents

TABLE OF CONTENTS

APPENDICES

Acknowledgments

MY SPECIAL THANKS ARE EXTENDED to the many designers, technicians, and actors that have graced my directing with their talent and inspired my creative work over the years. The Universities and professional theaters that provided a creative home for my directorial work deserve equal praise: Transylvania University, Florida State University, University of Pittsburgh, Three River's Shakespeare Festival, New City Theater, Regent University, and Saltworks Theater Company.

Bruce Long, executive director of Christians in Theater Arts, was again one of the first readers of my manuscript, offering much meaningful feedback and personal encouragement. Also, thanks to Mark Zillges who had the temerity to try the text out in his directing classes at Regent University. My wife, Betty Jo, who took time off from her creative work with fabric and painting to edit the text during its initial stages, deserves special praise and thanks.

I am especially grateful to our Lord, Jesus Christ, who in our lost-ness granted us the favor of being metaphor-makers under his Creative Mandate, and who ultimately made this project and the expressive arts, as a whole, possible.

Introduction

I DO NOT BELIEVE THERE IS SUCH a thing as Christian directing per se, though certainly the application of the leadership principles exemplified by Christ can inform personal and artistic choices that confront the director of stage plays. There is nothing Christian about learning the basic strengths and weaknesses of different types of stages, such as the proscenium stage versus theater-in-the-round. But the kind of communication needed to make the directing process a fruitful one can be greatly benefitted by the use of authority, sense of personal identity, and compassion that is exemplified in Jesus Christ.

The art of directing is more than getting a show produced. It is more than mastering stage movement, composition, imagery, and communication. Rather at the heart of direction is how you bring the resources of your own person to a process of creating art with other people. Essentially what you are is a mediator. You filter the talents and time of other artists through a text to discover truth. You are a servant to this process to communicate a cohesion of ideas, talents, and meaning directed toward a live audience. It is not all about you, it is about all of you. You need each other.

There comes a time in this process when you let go and say, "It is finished." You step back and watch as the unified vision of what everyone has contributed becomes a greater whole than the sum of its parts. The spirit of your combined efforts will hopefully result in a production that imparts truth that will work toward changing lives for the better by exploring the mystery of who we are and why we are called to play a part in God's Creative Mandate.

Ultimately, the world you have created will be torn down, the stage swept clean, and the auditorium will reverberate with a slight echo. You will move on with new images, words, phrases, and encounters that will contain the whisper of who you are and what you believe in. You are blessed to be able to work within the place of creativity; and you are doubly blessed by being equipped to bring not only your own resources, but those of your Creator into the directing process so that the gift of your Spiritual anointing can be shared with a cast of actors and technicians who will move onto their next play production having experienced the witness of Him through your artistic excellences and spirit of humility.

And this is what Jesus our Christ has modeled for us. In three short years he became the Father's work of art, which encompasses truth in himself and the image of this truth was further distributed by his disciples, i.e., his cast of characters who struggled, failed, and triumphed in passing on something eternal. Jesus became the Word incarnate, beautifully and intensely modeling the Kingdom of God in gesture, touch, words, images, and practice. Jesus is the truth, not just because he embodies the moral and ethical principles that reflect the truth of the Father, but because he literally embodies the truth through action: washing feet, feeding the hungry, healing the sick, embracing the broken and afraid, and allowing his head and feet to be anointed. He employs the world around him, olive trees, coins, bread, wine, wild waves, tears, and his breath as symbols of lasting significance. His Kingdom is not only ethereal but grounded in the day-to-day dust of our lives.

As a director, it is Jesus who should be your model for bringing significance to the mundane, loving even the least of those who work with and for you, and giving not merely who you are, but who you are in him.

Creating a work of art is about creating change. Art is brought into being in order that we might re-order what we see and respond to that which is around us in such a way that it becomes cast in a new and hopefully more meaningful, richer, and fuller light.

Lenora Inez Brown comments:

> I've always believed that religion and theatre have an almost interchangeable effect on the soul. When a play or production works, and I mean really works, one's spirit is uplifted and all that is confused seems clearer. Call it a cliché, but the experience of great theatre is religious. Characters speak to you—to the deepest part of your soul—and somehow the words make it easier to face the troubles of life and appreciate the happy moments more deeply.[1]

As a director, you are an artist blessed with the responsibility of creating something that will affect and perhaps change the consciousness of your cast, crew, and audience for the better. This is the redemptive shadow of all meaningful and well-executed aesthetic creations. Not all artwork does this. That is why your contribution and responsibility, as a faith-based artist who serves the Creator of all things, is to not glorify humankind's fallenness at the expense of what offers hope and points toward positive regeneration or change. Let your art be focused on change, for cultural betterment, and ultimately for furthering the Kingdom that is and that will be.

Theologian Walter Bruggeman, in his influential book *The Prophetic Imagination*, notes the roles of the prophet— the first of which is to lead the people in a shared public lament. Think of the Jewish people weeping over Ezra's reading of the Torah after the rebuilding of the wall and the temple. The prophet offers unique and challenging images and symbols to revitalize the community's awareness of their brokenness, hurt, and injustice. This time of communal anguish and criticism is followed by the prophet's second task, which is to present a vision of radical hope, a vision that frees us from the debilitating spirit of despair by providing a way out through the mystery of God's presence and redemption. What is to be learned here? The artist as prophet cannot shy away from addressing his community with images of our fallenness but has the additional responsibility of providing a new order, a vision for a world that reflects a redemptive positive light.[2]

You have adopted the mantle of storyteller. You tell other people's stories through the text that you are enlivening, and you also tell an aspect of your story through the interpretive process that you bring to this creative journey. There is a responsibility here to see the world as it is, but also to bring the most important and essential elements of who you are and what you believe into this artistic and leadership position. This is your footprint. This is your uniqueness. Use your uniqueness to say something that reflects your identity as a servant in his Kingdom.

Another responsibility that you have in terms of your witness of faith in our Creator is being good at what you do in the theatrical process. Really good. In a discipline that prides itself on following the dictates of moral relativism and political correctness, and which, to a degree, casts a biased look on those who profess to be adherents of Christianity, possessing rigorous leadership qualities as well as a lively artistic creativity is a must in establishing artistic and personal creditability. You are an ambassador for good art and a witness as a person of faith. Play your part well.

This book is loosely separated into two parts. Chapters 1–4 will focus on the role of the theater director, the leadership principles personified by Jesus in the Gospel of Luke, and the research and artistic constitution which are needed by the director to create a unified vehicle for the story. Chapters 5–8 examine more technically the skills needed by the director. This includes the nature of the beat, continues with script analysis, ground plan and central image concept, dialogue with designers, rehearsal process, and actor coaching.

Also, at the end of each chapter there are discussion questions and exercises to help you put into practice the lessons of each chapter.

Discussion Questions and Exercises

1. Read Bezalel's calling in Exodus (31:1–6). How does God use this craftsman in worship? How have you experienced the gift of the Holy Spirit as a guiding phenomenon in your artistic creations?

2. The Creative Mandate, as mentioned in the text, talks about the importance of us being blessed with the ability to make metaphors. How do you see this as an essential element in the artistic process? How is language metaphor? When Aristotle talks about the "imitation of an action," is he also talking about metaphor-making? How does a director use metaphor when talking to an actor? Provide some real or hypothetical examples.

3. Learning from Errors: I have perhaps learned more from my failures as a director than I have my more successful productions. Is this learning process something you can identify with in your artistic efforts? What did you learn from these experiences?

Chapter 1

Leadership and Directing Principles
from the Book of Luke

THERE IS OFTEN A GAP between the behavioral standards of Scripture and the ways in which we conduct our personal and public careers. This gap carries into our artistic efforts as well. Scriptural examples, however, do offer advice and instruction as to how to apply both aesthetic and communicative principles of action to our creative work and workplace disciplines.

Scripture is a wonderful resource to set a standard by which we measure the effectiveness of our personal disciplines. Through our continuing Bible study and our relationship with Christ we realize Jesus is a man of action. His words, his concerns, even his emotions inform us in terms of our own personal witness. They serve as a paradigm for our own sanctified walk that affects our work, our family relationships, and our devotions.

Various books and chapters in Scripture can serve as models for our creative and artistic endeavors. I always find time to dwell on God's calling to Bezalel in Exodus as a reminder of how God prepared, equipped, anointed, and blessed this artist and those around him with special creative and spiritual gifts (Exod. 31). The opening chapters of Genesis establish the aesthetic foundation of our calling as artists made in the image of God. It works like this: being made in God's image implies that God is an image maker. Since we are made in His image that makes us also image makers. Certainly, an attribute of this construct is that as image makers we have been gifted with the ability to construct metaphors. And this ability is an essential element of the creative process which I term the Creative Mandate. To somehow express the incredible nature of our Creator we can only use metaphors. In providing us with the written word, which in themselves are metaphors, our Lord has provided a diverse array of structure, imagery, and content as we look at the variety of genres revealed in Scripture: he uses poetry, dreams, historical drama, songs, fantasy, symbolism, and parables. You name it, it is there.

Personally, I have gone to Zechariah as an encouragement in learning not to despise small step by step beginnings as a creative artist. In a series of lectures, I have examined the book of Nehemiah as a paradigm for story structure. And I refer to the book of Joshua as an encouragement in confronting fear and stepping out into unknown creative territory.

Having directed scores of productions in the church, the academic, and the professional theater arenas, I have accumulated a lot of do's and don'ts that I try to adhere to in the process of choosing, directing, and producing a play. The first full length play I directed, fresh out of getting my MA in Theater from Tulane University, was the musical *110 in the Shade* (1963) at Fort Eustis, Virginia. Though the production was successful in terms of audience appreciation I knew where I had failed in terms of personal disciplines in establishing my position as director with the right kind of authority, by launching into a musical genre with no experience, and by not devising an artistic overlay that could carry the production in the small space on the base which we utilized—literally theater in an ex-barracks building. After the cast party, I went home and wrote a personal manifesto in which I swore not to make the same mistakes again, and I have not. Today I count my experiences where I have failed in some measure on a production as being of more helpful instructional value than the so-called successful productions.

In this chapter, I will overlay these experiences of successes and failures in the artistic realm with a look at Jesus as a model for the director, using the Gospel of Luke. Some of the examples will seem simplistic. Hopefully others will make you ponder. I would encourage you to think of your own experiences within the framework of the various Scriptures that I will be referencing. The emphasis is not on technical concerns such as blocking or composition in the examples I will provide, rather on the style of leadership and discipline concerning the relational aspects between the director and his staff and the individual actors.

On the Calling

"The Spirit of the Lord is upon me, because he has anointed me to bring good news to the poor. He has sent me to proclaim release to the captives and recovery of sight to the blind, to let the oppressed go free . . ."

—Luke 4:18 (NRSV)

When Jesus quoted from Isaiah in the verse above, he was publicly announcing that he had been given a calling: to tell the good news, to free prisoners, give sight to the blind, and to proclaim the coming of the King-dom. Have you been called to the art, i.e., to the business and creating of theater? Perhaps you have been called to teach, write, or perform. The theater is a precarious occupation so having the assurance of a calling is important in justifying that this is what you are to spend your time and talent in developing. If you are not sure, then you need to seek affirmation in prayer and in confirmation.

As a new and insecure Christian, aged thirty or so, and having just joined the theater faculty at the University of Pittsburgh, I struggled with the idea of continuing to work in the world of the theater. Is this what God called me to? How could I infuse my faith into my teaching, my directing, my writing—especially in a secular institution? Should I not go out into the desert someplace like Jesus, Paul, and others and focus on developing spiritual resources and a deeper relationship with God? Or maybe I should become a minister or missionary?

I prayed and received the following answer from 2 Timothy 3:14: "But as for you, continue in what you have learned . . ." (NRSV). And so, I was launched into the challenging world of trying to discover how I could become a witness to my faith in a secular arts context. It was and remains an ongoing challenge. I have failed at it in some areas, succeeded in others, but in looking back to hanging on by my spiritual nails, I know that this was my calling. During my years in Pittsburgh, I was able to find the time to begin to develop writing skills that later resulted in a substantial out-pouring of faith-based plays. I developed directing skills that launched me as a witness into a variety of professional directing forums. I co-founded Saltworks Theater Company, a professional organization that remains ac-tive today and which is staffed by administrators and theater talent who are believers in Jesus.

Remember, a calling is not just for you, but it is also for the Christian community that you are associated with, so always be looking for those connections. Sometimes the calling is not that clear. . . "I know Jesus wants me here, but why?" It most often is to prepare you for challenges that you will face in the artistic arena in the future. And know also, that as your calling becomes more and more recognized, significant, and shared, and as your skills and insights develop, it will also become ripe for attack by the forces of darkness. In fact, this is probably a sign which affirms that this is indeed what God has called you to.

Finally, as you work as a director under the call of the Lord of the

Universe, apply to it what might seem the smaller considerations of your art. Perhaps you are being called to start that company, to write that book, to become a spiritual giant in the creative world of the theater. Fine. But also apply your calling to the aspects of the plays you are directing. How do they reflect the beliefs which are at the center of your being? How can they become a witness to the community you are trying to communicate with? We all know the tremendous time and stress that goes into directing a play. There is nothing wrong in making commercial choices for financial gain. There is nothing wrong in selecting plays that are essentially comic romps: God created laughter so let's celebrate it. But at the end of your career when you look back, will you regret the choices you have made? My father was a noted and successful artist of worldwide fame, known primarily for his work in painting calendar girls. If you go to Google, you will find over 40,000 hits that address the name of Gil Elvgren. But he mentioned to me near the end of his life, "You know, I was given an exceptional artistic talent, and I wonder sometimes whether I used it in the right way. Maybe I should have branched out, tried more challenging and meaningful subject matter. Maybe. . ." Whatever your calling, it is going to be a challenge. It is going to have ups and downs, doubts, and triumphs. It is going to consume you as you progress deeper and deeper into it. Keep going back to the original call upon your life. Keep returning to the essence of God's calling which will hopefully result in a resounding: "His master said to him, 'Well done, good and trustworthy slave; you have been trustworthy in a few things, I will put you in charge of many things; enter into the joy of your master'" (Matt. 25:23, NRSV).

Build Your Work on the Rock

"As for everyone who comes to me and hears my words and puts them into practice, I will show you what they are like. They are like a man building a house, who dug down deep and laid the foundation on rock. When a flood came, the torrent struck that house but could not shake it, because it was well built. But the one who hears my words and does not put them into practice is like a man who built a house on the ground without a foundation. The moment the torrent struck that house, it collapsed, and its destruction was complete."

—Luke 6:47–49 (NIV)

If your play building process is built on rock, then you will have invited the Lord in to participate in the creative process and your house will be a place of refuge, of searching for personal and artistic truth, and a place of welcome. And you will have resisted the tides and waves that would pull it down which can be found in pride, hypocrisy, self-delusion, and commercially selling out. And finally, your house will be built aesthetically on the rock if you:

- Have done your beat work
- Have used your time wisely
- Have taken chances and dug deep within yourself to discover something new, and asked the question: in what way is my house unique and innovative?
- Have done your research

I think that research is one of the joys of being a director. It is the opportunity to become a minor expert in the areas of research within the perimeters of your play. Some examples from my experiences: in writing and directing *Brendan's Journey* (1993), I became well versed in early Irish history. In doing William Shakespeare's *The Merchant of Venice* (1605), I became quite knowledgeable about Jewish ghetto conditions in Venice during the late Medieval ages. Directing *Good* (1982) by C. P. Taylor resulted in my becoming informed about Nazi repression in World War II. Mounting a production of *The Frogs* (405 BC) by Aristophanes started me on a journey of investigating all kinds of exaggerated comedies, known as farces, throughout the ages. The skills required to master research should include being familiar with research search models, as well as with other artistic venues, and with a real curiosity and understanding of what has dramatic potential in both the spiritual and material worlds.

Authority

"Soon afterwards he went to a town called Nain, and his disciples and a large crowd went with him. As he approached the gate of the town, a man who had died was being carried out. He was his mother's only son, and she was a widow; and with her was a large crowd from the town. When the Lord saw her, he had compassion for her and said to her, 'Do not weep.' Then he came forward and touched the bier, and the bearers stood still. And he said, 'Young man, I say to you, rise!' The dead man sat up and began to speak, and Jesus gave him to his mother."

—Luke 7:11–15 (NRSV)

The widow's son is dead and Jesus instructs him to "Rise." Earlier he had told the widow in a sympathetic manner, "Don't cry." Jesus does not flatter. "Uh, if it's God's will, and, perhaps if you feel like it, and if it doesn't happen well, that's OK also." No, he goes right after what he wants and expects it to happen. I think this sort of directness is part of effective directing. Speak to the problem in a loving manner, and then provide a way out of it. Jesus spoke and then he acted. Action is the way to address the problem. Identify it and then act. That is the director's job. You have been gifted with discerning the problem and figuring out how to address it. Often, I have noted that something was not working and said something like this: "This moment isn't doing what it's supposed to do. We need to find another choice for Glenda to engage in getting her way with Harvey because that is what is driving the scene. Let's try this…" I knew a director who would discover a problem, send the cast home, and call them back several hours later once he had found the answer: morale was especially low. Do not be afraid of making a mistake because that will often lead to another more appropriate choice. The point is: take action!

Temptation

"Jesus, full of the Holy Spirit, returned from the Jordan and was led by the Spirit in the wilderness, where for forty days he was tempted by the devil."

—Luke 4:1–2 (NRSV)

Jesus goes off into the wilderness to meditate and prepare for the beginning of his public ministry. Your directing, for a period of several weeks, is going to test you in all sorts of ways artistically and personally. So you should be a front-line prayer warrior for your play production process.

Jesus meditated on Scripture. Do the same, and select verses that emphasize the disciplines of patience, perseverance, and perception. In directing a production of Christopher Marlowe's *Doctor Faustus* (1592), I gleaned numerous quotes from Scripture concerned with spiritual warfare and equipping ourselves for battle with the enemy and read them daily to the cast. This was because the play itself features dark ritual practices as well as demonic characters.

In addition, keep reading over your script and what you are directing as late in the process as you can. When directing Shakespeare, I discipline myself to re-read and re-study the scenes that I will be directing each day. The script is your source, so honor it. English actor and director Lawrence Olivier was noted for his consistent return to the script, and he attributed the discovery of new ideas and approaches to scenic moments to this habit.

In the wilderness, Jesus was tempted by needs of the flesh, thirst, and hunger, and was tested emotionally through Satan's offering him inordinate power and glory. What are some of the temptations that can confront you as a director? Perhaps not by food but certainly by the flesh. As a director your position is one of preeminence in this artistic endeavor. What you say goes, and this position of power can be exploited by using it for self-ish ends, especially in terms of sexual license. Do not be led astray in this way. No good can come from it and it is a denial of your faith foundation. The theater and film environments are intense experiences, demanding great sacrifices of time and expectations on your abilities. As such, one can be emotionally vulnerable and led into relationships that can only end in destructive behavior between individuals and the artistic integrity of the work. In other words, do not use your position of power to do anything more than enhance the quality of the work and the productive relationships between individuals.

This power syndrome can also be abused by demanding things to be exclusively your way, by taking the glory when it belongs to the Lord as well as to the communal process, and by being threatened by input from other people. Zechariah 4:6 says, "Not by might, nor by power, but by my Spirit, says the Lord" (NRSV).

Jesus was fearless in facing the powers of the enemy with his knowl-edge of the Word and his ability to discern the motivations of the Lord of Darkness. Our insecurities can lead to us creating or giving in to power trips to cover up these fears. This results in closing ourselves off from other human beings because we do not want to accept their critical input. We can blame others for what is seemingly going wrong with the production process. And we can cover up this insecurity with outbursts of temper which keep us from examining our inner selves and oftentimes facing a truth that we do not want to face. To avoid this, we can be open to the input from others and consider it honestly. Always question your motives by arming yourself with verses from Scripture in areas that you know you are vulnerable. I would also suggest having a mentor figure that you trust and could go to for sharing prayer, problems, and receiving personal and creative counseling.

The Proof Is in the Pudding

"One of the Pharisees asked Jesus to eat with him, and he went into the Pharisee's house and took his place at the table. And a woman in the city, who was a sinner, having learned that he was eating in the Pharisee's house, brought an alabaster jar of ointment. She stood behind him at his feet, weeping, and began to bathe his feet with her tears and to dry them with her hair. Then she continued kissing his feet and anointing them with the ointment. Now when the Pharisee who had invited him saw it, he said to himself, 'If this man were a prophet, he would have known who and what kind of woman this is who is touching him—that she is a sinner.'"

—Luke 7:36–39 (NRSV)

This woman at the Pharisee's house shows real courage through her emotional vulnerability and actions as she cries and dries the tears on his feet with her hair. Then she kisses his feet and pours perfume on them. Here we have a demonstration of the absolute beauty of gesture. Sometimes we depend too much on the spoken words. In theater, we have the acting technique *gestus*, developed by German theater director Bertolt Brecht, which is a combination of body language, facial expression, and gestures, and also the archetypal gestural approach to acting of Michael Chekhov.[1] Both techniques are often what we are looking for to crystallize an action so that it transcends the moment and is so emotionally charged that it remains unforgettable. This woman's gesture resonates with us even as we read it, by itself, isolated from the rest of Scripture. It takes a moment through a gesture and universalizes its implications. It combines emotion and love and beauty and total commitment beyond what we could imagine. It is another way of speaking truth.

The next moment is the exact antithesis of this. Here, the Pharisee who is watching says to himself: "If this man really were a prophet, he would know what kind of woman is touching him. He would know that she is a sinner" (Luke 7:39, CEV). This criticism stands in stark contradiction to the silent, gestural moment of truth between Jesus and the prostitute. The Pharisee's reaction is judgmental, small-minded, culturally specific, and limiting. It puts God in a box.

Jesus knows the man's thoughts. He responds with a story, with art. What he says in the narrative teaches and convicts: "A certain creditor had two debtors: one owed five hundred denarii, and the other fifty. When they could not pay, he canceled the debts for both. Now which of them will love him more?" (Luke 7:41–42, NRSV).

The people then hear Jesus say: "Your sins are forgiven." Shocking. They ignore her sacrifice, they ignore His saving grace, they only respond with outrage. Good Christians do not allow themselves to feature prostitutes in their plays or films, right? Hopefully you are not creating under this sort of self-imposed censorship. Go for the beauty. Go for the gestural truth. Let the moment speak for itself.

Seeing the Big Picture

"Once when Jesus was praying alone, with only the disciples near him, he asked them, 'Who do the crowds say that I am?' They answered, 'John the Baptist; but others, Elijah; and still others, that one of the ancient prophets has arisen.' He said to them, 'But who do you say that I am?' Peter answered, 'The Messiah of God.'"

—Luke 9:18–20 (NRSV)

Peter was able to see the big picture. That is the job of the director. Actors scramble around in their moments. Directors are putting all the pieces together so that they represent something greater than the sum of the parts.

Directors are concerned with processes: in rhythm, in builds, with repetitions of actions, with complicated imagery. Too often the beginning director will say things like, "I don't like it when you move to the sofa" or "I don't believe it when you pick up the knife." They are noticing something is wrong, but they are not describing it in terms of the bigger picture. Rather, try this: "The move to the sofa doesn't seem to be working because she has spent a good part of the first act avoiding this guy and for her to go to him before his revelation in the next scene would give away and undercut their reconciliation which will take place later." Or: "As an actor you picked the knife up as if your character had done it like this every day, but today she is thinking about suicide so that every object she handles should have a quality that makes it a potential suicide weapon."

It is the director's job to know each nuanced moment in the script and to understand how each new scene builds on the previous one to form an image of the whole.

Do It, Why Not?

"Just then a man from the crowd shouted, 'Teacher, I beg you to look at my son; he is my only child. Suddenly a spirit seizes him, and all at once he shrieks. It convulses him until he foams at the mouth; it mauls him and will scarcely leave him. I begged your disciples to cast it out, but they could not.' Jesus answered, 'You faithless and perverse generation, how much longer must I be with you and bear with you? Bring your son here.' While he was coming, the demon dashed him to the ground in convulsions. But Jesus rebuked the unclean spirit, healed the boy, and gave him back to his father. And all were astounded at the greatness of God."

—Luke 9: 38–43 (NRSV)

In this case Jesus demonstrates to his disciples the faith principles of healing and of dealing with the enemy. We are told in the theater as directors: "Direct from the audience. Don't ever 'show' your actors what to do or how to do it. No line readings please." Jesus did not stop at this moment to provide an instructional lesson to his disciples in the finer art of exorcism. Direct action was needed, otherwise time would have been wasted, and the demon could have further harmed the boy.

I inform my actors at the onset of a production that now and then I will get on stage and work through how a prop might be manipulated or a movement made. I do this only when I literally must explore the moment myself to understand, as an actor within the context of a character, how this moment can work. I do it when I cannot come up with the motivational words that will communicate effectively what the moment needs. I never say "do it like me," but I experiment. I demonstrate a process that hopefully the actor will pick up and respond to and make their own. I do not say the lines as such but improvise so the energy of the moment is communicated.

You might say I am breaking all the rules, but I have rarely been reprimanded for this, more often I am thanked by the actor for helping to discover immediate possibilities in making the moment happen. When working with new actors, being on the stage, and walking through movement and lines with them can cut time from the rehearsal process, and even provide them with confidence, but do not linger there.

Do not talk laboriously about how a moment or a line might need fixing. A gesture, a tone of voice, energy communicated, action in space can tell the story and remedy the situation more than a lot of verbal nonsense where you become more interested in not threatening the creative impulse of the actor at the expense of getting something done.

My discipline extends to trying not to give an actor a line reading but rather communicating the energy and verbal possibilities through my reactions to a moment that is not working. If this fails, in the last few days of rehearsal before technical rehearsals begin, I will inform the actor that I am providing a line reading and that I want it done this way for this reason. The only caution here is that you, as a director, need to have enough acting chops to be able to deliver the line or movement effectively. I have done this with both professional and university actors. I also try and couch this within the framework of praising them for a character revelation in an adjacent moment or for something that is working because it reveals the truth of the moment.

Play Selection: The Essence of Our Worldview

"Those who are ashamed of me and of my words, of them the Son of Man will be ashamed when he comes in his glory and the glory of the Father and of the holy angels."
—Luke 9:26 (NRSV)

One of our struggles as believing artists is to try and figure out how to bring together our beliefs with authenticity and truth in terms of story and dramatic action. We spend a lot of time arguing and sweating over justifications for our work as redeemable. What does this word "redeemed" mean to you? Redeemed from what? Redeemed into what? Redeemed by whom? What is the distinction between feeling good from a happy ending versus the forgiveness and fellowship that stem from true redemption?

The process of theater and the role of the director is built on more than play selection. Several artistic relationships are formed during a play production process, and all of them are enriched by the Christian virtues that establish an effective witness in a leadership role. However, play selection is where the process of production begins.

I have mainly worked in a university theater environment, with extended ventures into church and professional theater from that base. The plays I have selected to do for university audiences reflect the fact that I am working within the context of an MFA program where it is required and needed that a wide selection of classical works be offered: the Greeks, Shakespeare, Realism, Epic, American classic, musicals, and so forth. Hopefully, but too often rarely, this should also include original works. If I was exclusively a Broadway director or worked only within community theater, the extent of my choices would be more focused on the needs and audiences of those venues.

The Christian director is also somewhat limited in the selection of works which reflect her faith not only because of the theater structure she is working for, but also because of the limited audiences and scripts which embrace a more direct Christian witness. So would we be compromising our witness by mounting a production of *Our Town* (1938), or *A Funny Thing Happened on the Way to the Forum* (1962), or *Equus* (1973)? I do not think so, but there will always be Christian audience members who will question your choices from their selective theological viewpoints. *Our Town* presents a questionable representation of the after-death quandary; *Forum* features dancing prostitutes and sexual humor; *Equus* has nudity. There is nothing wrong with celebrating the great major and minor works of the world's dramatic *oeuvre*, or body of work, but where does that leave you as a believer?

The process of play selection is a challenging one. I was gently criticized for directing Harold Pinter's *Old Times* (1971). It is a brilliant play. I think it is Pinter's best. It is a study of a decaying marriage, with one of the partners slipping into delusional insanity and the other desperate to find out why and trying to stop it. The subject matter does not promote a sinful lifestyle and there is no attack on or introduction of religious subject matter. It does not promote a redemptive message or even offer an avenue of hope. However, I count it as seminal in terms of my development as a director and my understanding of the forceful and even lyrical use of subtext. In writing *Paper Wings* (1995), a two-person play that deals with the family dynamics of what happened when my mother became a

Christian and my father fought against it, the use of subtext became an important element in expanding the conflict dynamic. Subtext is what is not said, or the broader implications of what someone really means when they say something. Having directed several of Pinter's plays, I learned to appreciate the diverse use of language that he has mastered. We learn from the masters. Bezalel most likely learned his craft in Egypt under Egyptian craftsmen, the best in the world, before God anointed him as the main artisan to build the Ark of the Covenant and other worship artifacts for the tent of meeting (Exod. 31).

Directing Shakespeare equipped me to better understand and appreciate the power of language as action. Almost every play that I have directed promotes a positive message that I would categorize as being proactively virtuous to some degree or other. You as an individual are a combined force of talents and experiences that the Lord is preparing for something unique and innovative in terms of promoting your faith and values to a fallen world. What is needed are writers and directors who, like Bezalel, have been trained and gained experience from the best in the business, and who are able to bring their mature Christian faith into their artistic expression in the most challenging ways possible.

The director, through interpretive selection, can shape the meaning of a play in ways that emphasize the dire straits of the character's fall from grace. For example, in a show I directed of Henrik Ibsen's *Peer Gynt* (1876), to emphasize the titular character's fall from grace at the end of a production, I showed Peer Gynt, this world traveler, this man of worldly ideas and appetites broken, peeling an onion, shedding his clothes, weeping from the onion tears of despair, only barely cognizant of the goodness that he left behind in the character of Solveig, who is now blind. It is too late. I also added the character of death with a scythe waiting to take him the rest of the way on his journey.

Frank Burch Brown in his important book *Good Taste, Bad Taste, and Christian Taste* talks about negative transcendence. He makes a case for the power of literature and film that ends depicting such an extended negative state of existence for characters and situations that the reader or audience is convinced of the need not to end up in a similar state. And thus, might begin a search for hope and light in a lost world.[2] As a director, I use this approach as a tool when directing plays that depict an absence of personal salvation. The musical *Cabaret* (1966) ends with Sally Bowles singing the theme song, having had an abortion, and with her love, Cliff, on his way back to America. She has sold out to the lure of the Kit Kat Club and to the sensual temptations of encroaching Nazism. My concept had the Master of Ceremonies manipulating her like a puppet from above during this final moment. In *Waiting for Godot* (1952) by Samuel Beckett, I had the main characters Gogo and Didi become ciphers lobotomized in a lost sense of individual histories. And in Cecil Taylor's *Good* (1982), Professor Halder, a student of German writer and scientist Goethe, becomes a Nazi automaton standing at the gates of Auschwitz deciding who lives or dies. Witnessing how far man can fall down the ladder of expectations of civilized behavior becomes a moral lesson that can hopefully lead to a response toward redemption from the audience.

Other moments in more positive play endings can be celebrated. How to play the ending of Shakespeare's *King Lear* (c. 1606) when Edgar says, "Look up" as Lear's soul seems to ascend? What an opportunity. In Christopher Marlowe's *Doctor Faustus* (c. 1592) when the demons of hell open the pit to receive the professor, Faustus looks up deciding whether to embrace a single saving drop of Christ's blood or not. I tried to make this a definitive action, not just a line of dialogue. In Scripture Joseph is a recognizable Christ figure. What can you do to reflect this in *Joseph and the Amazing Technicolor Dreamcoat* (1969)? The same can be said for Don Quixote in *The Man from La Mancha* (1965). In a stage adaptation I wrote of Geoffrey Chaucer's *Canterbury Tales* (c. 1400) I have the various characters arrive at the Cathedral and each make a plea before the altar based on the tales they told in Chaucer's text. The following is good Constance's prayer which I added to the play:

> CONSTANCE: Oh Lord of light, I've traveled far,
> And seen the dark face of man's desire,
> Who from grace has fallen, like a shooting star,
> To be consumed by hate and envy and ire.
> I ask that on my last and fateful journey,
> Your breath will be my wind, your tears my sea,
> Your hand to rescue this poor refugee,
> And to your Son my Savior I plead,
> That he will be my vessel, my ship indeed,
> And hasten my trip with all Godspeed.[3]

My final note on this complicated subject which could bear a great deal more explanation is this: everyone is going to stand before God's throne and give an account of their lives. God will have met everyone during their brief sojourn on this planet and have offered them the choice to accept and follow Him. As a universal experience, everyone will have gone through it; so to not consider the person and realm of God and his Kingdom as relevant and meaningful material for your dramatic efforts is a kind of denial. The challenge, of course, is to break new ground in discovering approaches to the vast riches of our spiritual heritage found in Scripture, found in the history of the saints, and hopefully manifesting itself in your own artistic sensibilities. Capture the essence and feel of the following verse in your creative imagination: "Therefore, if anyone is in Christ, the new creation has come. The old has gone, the new is here" (2 Cor. 5:17, NIV).

Listening and Responding with a Question

"And then a voice came from the cloud, saying, 'This is My Son, My Chosen One; listen to Him!'"

—Luke 9:35 (NASB)

During Jesus's transfiguration, the disciples, who were getting it all wrong, were told, "This is my chosen son. Listen to Him!" (Luke 9:35, NAB). How often did they not listen? When are they going to get the point? For, "faith comes from what is heard, and what is heard comes through the word of Christ" (Rom. 10:17, NRSV). I know that I tend to repeat myself when giving directorial criticism. Better to say it once, and then ask the actors whether they understand what you are talking about. Learn to converse with them; do not lecture them. Your tone of voice is important. You do not want your actors to feel berated, manipulated, or that you are becoming impatient with them. Everything in the production may appear to be falling apart, except for you and the measured tones and insights you provide in stressful situations. It is important not to overload the actors. When you give a note, if possible, work it out on stage right after you give it. It takes more time, so leave more time, because the working through of a note will anchor it in the actor's mind.

A technical note such as crossing on a particular line, or altering when a prop is picked up, as well as complimentary moments, can and should be shared with the entire ensemble in a note session. If you have a note that is more personal always try to get the actor in a one-on-one moment when you share your concerns.

When Jesus was in the temple as a child, he asked questions and listened. During his ministry when he was asked a question he would often respond with a question in turn. When an actor comes to you with a question, often they already have a sense of what the answer is, but they want assurance, attention, and of course further understanding. It is also a mechanism to avoid future criticism: "if I can get the director to tell me what to do, and it doesn't work, then it won't be my fault." So, ask them in turn what they think. This gives them the opportunity to express what is really going on inside. Perhaps the issue is not so much a motivational moment for the character as much as an opportunity for the actor to express something more personal that is going on within himself. Also, if you ask, "well, what do you think the character is thinking here and what would he do?" when the actor responds with a choice, she has made it her own and her artistic confidence will be increased. It is your job now to try out the choice in rehearsal.

Usually I find that two-thirds of the way through the rehearsal process the actors begin to know more about the character they are playing than I do. Listen carefully and watch closely the choices they make because they will be coming from a creative well-spring that is essential and formative to the life of the character and the transformation of the actor.

The relationship of Mary and Martha toward each other and Jesus illuminates terms of listening and reacting (Luke 10:18–41). Actors and technicians will often measure their performances or jobs in relation to how much work they feel they are putting out as compared to the amount of work they feel others are doing. This leads to being judgmental. How easy it is to get caught up in the mundane and the everyday. Servants like Martha are essential, but there is a spirit of busyness about them. Worry and perhaps jealousy and a little bit of anger cause Martha to accuse her sister. She totally misses what Jesus is saying. She misses the forest for the trees. She jeopardizes a sisterly relationship with a critical spirit.

Toward tech week, the final week of rehearsals with all the technical proponents like lights and sound cues added, you will be inundated with a thousand choices and a plethora of details. Do not rush. Listen to people. Martha felt that she was doing things by herself, that she was not being recognized for what she was doing. She needed and wanted attention. So be sure to spread your attention liberally and help people to really listen to each other.

Faithful and Unfaithful Servants

"And the Lord said, 'Who then is the faithful and prudent manager whom his master will put in charge of his slaves, to give them their allowance of food at the proper time?'"

—Luke 12:42 (NRSV)

It is your responsibility to know what each person under your direction is supposed to do. If not, you run the risk of being taken advantage of. Know what the costumer expects. An example: most costume designers dislike dress parades because they are often parading costume bits and pieces and it takes up a lot of valuable time. If you stick your head in the costume shop, they are usually quite open to showing you what they are working on, and a great deal can be accomplished then. Know how to look at elevations for lighting setups and prop designs and how to create and read *ground plans*, which show the birds-eye-view of the set drawn to scale. These are the cornerstones of your creation, so launching out in rehearsal without having mastered these documents and their interpretation is a hinderance to everyone. When you realize that you have been working on a taped floor plan of a set that does not represent what is on the ground plan, and you need an extra two feet downstage that is not there, that is where trouble begins.

And what about the music director? Can you read music? If not, learn. Are you sensitive enough to lyrics and musical movements that you can effectively direct a singer to embody the essence of a song? You might not be choreographing large numbers, but you will be coaching single and small cast song numbers. Does your choreographer really understand the dramatic requisites of the number? Have you created a ground plan for a musical number that tells the story as well as serves the performers in terms of movement and prop requirements?

Schedule weekly or bi-weekly production meetings and prepare for them with notes and questions. Take notes at these meetings and be sure to distribute them in a timely fashion to your support and design staff. Visit often individual designers and technical assistants in their workspaces. Show that you are interested and get them to discuss problems and concerns. Jesus was there for the community of people who followed and depended upon him. Be there for your staff and company members.

Your *stage manager* should be your most faithful servant. It is expected of you, therefore, to know the responsibilities and rules of stage managing. Make sure that you go over these responsibilities in a one-on-one meeting before the production begins its rehearsals. If there is one person with whom you need to have ongoing communication and understanding, it is your stage manager. Some of the disciplines of relationship and communication I try and maintain are as follows:

- Communicate after every rehearsal with your stage manager. Go over notes that you have given her, and double check on technical, design, and administrative communications needed for the upcoming rehearsals and meetings.

- Do not be shy about asking her opinion concerning certain directorial choices that you have made. Often stage managers are prospective directors and will have valuable insights. This also provides them with the sense that they are valued on several different levels.

- Be sure that she funnels any artistic opinions through you. Actors should never be directing other actors, or even making public suggestions to you concerning artistic choices. Make sure anyone who wants to contribute an idea goes to the stage manager or to you on a break moment.

- Your stage manager will often hear and know about personal and professional concerns that individual designers, technicians, and actors are having with the process of your directorial approach. Listen and respond to your stage manager's observations and suggestions.

- Let the stage manager know how you work insofar as blocking is concerned—your particular working method. This is very important. Often a stage manager will have preconceived notions of how blocking rehearsals should be conducted. Because I rarely pre-block, the result is that my rehearsal process is somewhat free flowing, with experimentation and blocking changes happening up until close to tech week. I do not always accomplish all that the schedule for any particular rehearsal period is anticipating. In one instance, I had a stage manager who could not work under these conditions, and the result was a total breakdown in communication. Be sure to obtain a manual on the duties of a stage manager and really get to know its contents.

"All You Need Is Love"

"But I say to you that listen, love your enemies, do good to those who hate you, bless those who curse you, pray for those who abuse you."

—Luke 6:27–28 (NRSV)

"He answered, 'You shall love the Lord your God with all your heart, and with all your soul, and with all your strength, and with all your mind; and your neighbor as yourself.'"

—Luke 10:27 (NRSV)

Creative arts activities can be very self-oriented. Your imagination is on the line, your creative impulses are being judged by the public and by your fellow artists. Your creation is related to the very essence of who you are, what you stand for and believe, and as such is personalized as an aspect of you. Other fields such as accounting, most of the sciences, and a great deal of manufacturing create a product which is essentially neutral in terms of a personal signature. Theater, by its very nature of finding truth in character and action, is subjective, involves a personal sense of identification, and is driven by giving form to feeling as Susan Langer has written in *Feeling and Form*.[4] The standards by which we measure truth in this arts continuum are personalized by the approach, background, training, and worldview of the director.

The director in the theatrical process plays the role of a mini-god. At her command people move, talk, and behave according to her interpretation of the life of the script. She is the one who literally says "let there be light" here and there, all at her request. Her interpretative stamp is usually on every production. It is easy to let this go to one's head, and to become the only central and driving force of the production.

I have heard directors boast of driving actors to despair and tears to break down artistic pre-conceptions. I have heard them rant at actors, telling them that they have no understanding of the character or the acting process. Some directors may feel that they must be perfect, that they cannot make mistakes. You give notes criticizing actors and dramatic moments for several weeks, but there is no one charged with critiquing your work. The result of this can be an affected air of superiority, of obsessive ownership over the creative production, and a deafness to legitimate criticism. As I have said before, every actor is encouraged to find something they can love about the character they are playing, and in the same way every director should strive to find something they can love about the actors and the crew that they are working with.

The good director must be other-oriented. You are as much a psychologist as you are an artistic strategist. As a leader, you are melding a disparate group of talented individuals into a living product in which the whole will generate meaning and beauty and truth which goes far beyond the traits of any single individual and creates a unity and a whole which is greater than the sum of all these particular and wonderful parts. Think of what Christ pulled together as his ensemble: fisherman, tax collectors, prostitutes, a Pharisee, a Zealot/revolutionary, a thief, and perhaps some tradesmen. It was through love that he was able to form them into a group that would radically change the world's spiritual landscape. Nobody knew the proclivities of these men better than Jesus. He taught them, demonstrated for them, provided them with narratives, chastised them, and above all gave them a vision for love that was and is the foundational cornerstone for the Gospel. Jesus set a standard that is almost impossible to emulate, but when practiced can have positive effects on your rehearsal process and artistic creation.

Present your criticism in terms of the character and the bigger picture of the play. Avoid using the word "I" in terms of what you are looking for. Do not say, "I want you to sit on the word 'relax,'" or "I want you to do it this way," or "I want you to be angrier." It is not you who wants, it is the play and the character and the moment which demands. Use the plural "us" or "let's"—"Let's see if you can find the moment in which you collapse, to just get away, somewhere during this beat." "Let's explore some more possibilities that make you conclude you have to slap him in the face." "Right now, you're just displaying anger toward Gertrude. Anger never just exists by itself; it comes from someplace else, often it is something not being said. Let's see if we can find that." What you are communicating is that you are in this together, that the problem is an artistic one, not a personal one. That's a statement of love.

In a professional production I directed of Shakespeare's *All's Well That Ends Well* (1623), one of the actors who played a minor comic character felt the need to direct vocally those around him and to make directorial suggestions toward the cast. This must be stopped immediately, but how to do that with love? I took the actor aside and told him that I appreciated his passion and insights but that it was not his job to make them public, especially by making directorial suggestions to those around him. I told him to bring his ideas to the stage manager or to me during a break for us to consider. I did use a few of his ideas, and I made sure that I let the cast know where the ideas came from as I incorporated them into the production.

In the premiere production of Leon Katz's *A Death at Astapovo* (1980), I noticed an ensemble actor's energy seemed to be waning. In talking with him he explained that he had been working like a dog on this small part and never received any feedback from me. I apologized and went over my positive assessment of his work up to that point, and he left satisfied. I realized that I had taken his work for granted. Actors need the director's attention. A side note: when giving feedback to actors, do not say, "You're doing a great job, keep it up." That might be better than nothing, but it is not what the actor needs. You need to notice a moment that really works and express why you feel it is working so well for the character. "You know when everyone is clamoring up the steps, and you sort of drag, and hang on the railing? What made you make that choice?" He explains. You respond. "Great instincts at work. Stay in touch with where that came from, there's truth there."

This is true for not only the actors, but the crew also. If a follow spot, or spotlight, operator is quick on the learning curve, let him know you have noticed. The scimitar that the prop designer made is perfect; describe how it works so well in rehearsal. And thank them. If you personally learn something from someone, tell them and thank them.

I had a student actor who was disconsolate, interruptive, rude, and argumentative. I tried every strategy I knew, even to the point of contemplating taking him out of the production. Finally, and I should have done this much earlier, I prayed: "Lord, I'm having real problems even liking this guy, but I know you love him. Help me here to find what's wrong and help me to address it." Almost immediately God provided to me the feeling of what this student was going through personally, and the pain that he felt almost overwhelmed me. I was able to relate to him on a different and more compassionate level, and almost overnight the production discipline problems disappeared. So, keep up an active prayer life concerning all aspects of the process and invite our Heavenly Father to become an active participant.

Excuses: The Cost of Following Jesus

"As they were going along the road, someone said to him, 'I will follow you wherever you go.' And Jesus said to him, 'Foxes have holes, and birds of the air have nests; but the Son of Man has nowhere to lay his head.' To another he said, 'Follow me.' But he said, 'Lord, first let me go and bury my father.' But Jesus said to him, 'Let the dead bury their own dead; but as for you, go and proclaim the kingdom of God.' Another said, 'I will follow you, Lord; but let me first say farewell to those at my home.' Jesus said to him, 'No one who puts a hand to the plow and looks back is fit for the kingdom of God.'"

—Luke 9: 57–62 (NRSV)

The above passage describes humankind's propensity to intend to do something and then find an excuse for not doing it. From a directing standpoint, some of the excuses so often put forth are:

- Not being well prepared overall on a rehearsal-by-rehearsal basis. Spend an hour a day briefing yourself on what you want to accomplish in that day's rehearsal.

- Not confronting and promptly addressing personality problems between you and the cast or among cast members. Communicate.

- Blaming other people for things going wrong: "the actors didn't do what I told them." It is easy to blame failure on difficult actors, on technical glitches, on too little time, or a lack of talent. Take on responsibility for mistakes; try to mitigate the problems.

As a director, what does it mean to take up one's cross? It means being willing to pay the cost from the standpoint of time commitment and preparation. It means taking personal responsibility for your actions and words in and out of the rehearsal process. It means going the extra mile in being sensitive to the emotional and creative struggles of the actors. They are the ones who are faced with the response of a live audience.

Keeping the Calm

"And while they were sailing, he fell asleep. A windstorm swept down on the lake, and the boat was filling with water, and they were in danger. They went to him and woke him up, shouting, 'Master, Master, we are perishing!' And he woke up and rebuked the wind and the raging waves; they ceased, and there was a calm. He said to them, 'Where is your faith?' They were afraid and amazed, and said to one another, 'Who then is this, that he commands even the winds and the water, and they obey him?'"

—Luke 8: 23–25 (NRSV)

It is difficult to think of a production that does not have some moments of panic, from learning lines to technical glitches, to the pressure of the approaching opening, to burgeoning insecurity over choices, the list goes on. I directed Shakespeare's *Much Ado About Nothing* (1623) for an equity company and the buzz was that Elvgren's concept was not going to work, that the actors were being asked to pull off the impossible, that certain scenes would not be humorous, and that the actors would look foolish. A small group representing the cast approached me three days before we opened to discuss cuts and changes. I listened to their concerns, but assured them that it was all coming together, and to forge ahead with the concept and schedule that we had originally laid out. When the production opened, they were amazed at the universal responses from the audience in terms of catching the concept and being swept up by the story and the various comic elements. And though I might have had some personal doubts, I appeared calm, assured, and exuded confidence. Unlike Jesus's manipulation of the elements, there was nothing miraculous about the final results; but like Jesus, the director needs to be the quiet center of the storm in any production.

Hopefully you know Jesus as your calm center and that his Spirit is beside you as you journey across the seas of panic and doubt. If you lose your calm, it can seriously undermine your creditability and authority. Do not do it. Remember, you are the one that is seeing the forest, not just the trees. As director, your task is to bring a visionary skill set that is the guiding light for the production.

Many years ago I directed a huge production of a play I authored entitled *Steel/City* (1976). Two weeks before we opened, we were still in the process of massive rewrites and cuts, which can be a discombobulating experience for everyone. The producer and co-author came up to me in the middle of a rehearsal and said, "Elvgren, how can you stay so calm? It must be that faith thing of yours." Holding onto your faith strongholds can be a true witness in times of distress and challenge.

Emulation

"A disciple is not above the teacher, but everyone who is fully qualified will be like the teacher."

—Luke 6:40 (NRSV)

As director, whether you like it or not, you are the model to be emulated.

From the production concept to the agendas for meetings, the rehearsal schedule and breakdown of timing requirements, these will determine the tenor and tone of your production disciplines. You are the one responsible, and the entire creative community will be looking to you for guidance and the setting of certain standards. So, what do they follow?

First, consider your discipline and organization. Always get to rehearsals before they are scheduled to start to double check space, props, and to talk with actors before the action begins. If you are late, they will begin to be late. Watch your language. Do not reduce your expressiveness to berating. Do not be involved with gossip or share your opinion of an actor's capability with other actors or stage crew. Help set the performance space up if you are inclined. Disciplines that you establish will be copied and picked up by those around you.

Regarding scheduling rehearsals, it is very important that you utilize the time of actors, especially in early rehearsals, with as much efficiency as possible. Call people for certain times that maximizes their involvement, so they are not sitting around the theater or green room for endless hours waiting to enter for a short scene rehearsal. Always try to get through your schedule for the day, because actors want to feel that they are being utilized, respected, and are progressing. If this means scheduling text moments out of a linear context, do it. Your sensitivity here will be appreciated and hopefully copied.

All That Praise—Bring It On!

"Woe to you when all speak well of you."

—Luke 6: 26 (NRSV)

You are in for trouble when everyone says good things about you.

Listen to praise sparingly. Theater people crave this and give it out unsparingly. Do not be satisfied. The show is never ready. Do not get fooled by good reviews and complimentary statements. You should know what is wrong with your show. You know what artistic moments do not work; you know where you compromised; you know where you have alienated another human being. One of my fears is that I will let artistic praise cloud my critical judgement, and that I will believe that I have directed a successful show, when it is not as good as I think it is. This happens because of listening and taking to heart too much praise.

At the same time, we all need affirmation. God says to Jesus at his baptism, "You are my own dear son, and I am pleased with you" (Luke 3:22,

CEV). Does this imply that Jesus needs affirmation? It could be, I am not sure. But it never hurts. Do we need affirmation? All the time. I still look for affirmation from other artists. Hopefully I can also receive with humility negative criticism. As I have mentioned before, in giving affirmation to an actor do not deal with generalizations, be specific about selective moments and choices in their acting work.

A Bunch of Woes

"But woe to you Pharisees! For you tithe mint and rue and herbs of all kinds, and neglect justice and the love of God; it is these you ought to have practiced, without neglecting the others."
—Luke 11:42 (NRSV)

Are you cheating on the valuable time that you need to give to God? What do you feel you are giving back to God in terms of the directing work you are doing? Are you continuing to seek him out and give him the credit that is his due? Do you continue to invite him into your process of directorial choices and interactions?

"Now you Pharisees clean the outside of the cup and of the dish, but inside you are full of greed and wickedness."—Luke 11:39 (NRSV)

Are you playing a role, what are you hiding?

"Woe to you Pharisees! For you love to have the seat of honor in the synagogues and to be greeted with respect in the marketplaces."—Luke 11:43 (NRSV)

Are you a name dropper? Do you look for adoration in the wrong places? Are you swayed by popular opinion?

"Woe also to you lawyers! For you load people with burdens hard to bear, and you yourselves do not lift a finger to ease them."—Luke 11:46 (NRSV)

On a film set in New England the actor David Strathearn was working for a director friend of mine who told me that David never neglected to help the grips and gaffers unload the trucks when they were on location at a film shoot. Are you one to help your crew when the going gets challenging physically?

"Woe to you! For you build the tombs of the prophets whom your ancestors killed."—Luke 11:47 (NRSV)

Are you concerned about what your legacy is going to be? What do you want written on your tombstone? Hopefully it goes something like this: "I worked hard, I sought the truth, and I loved the Lord my God." You realize, of course, that the theater art is a fleeting one; that the final performance is followed by the tearing down of the set and of dust settling on an empty stage. Are you putting what counts, loving the Lord with all your will, soul, and might and your fellowman as yourself, as the final culmination of your work here on earth? Some artists try and ensure their immortality through their artwork. A colleague of mine boldly declared that "Theater is my God." Get your priorities straight. You are constantly on display as a master teacher and mature artist. Do not hinder those who apprentice beneath you, nor become a stumbling block; let your witness be strong, share what you know, unstintingly, especially what you know about the Lord.

Discussion Questions and Exercises

1. **Build Your Work on the Rock**: What does it mean to really build you creative work on the principles and faith in Christ?

   - **Disciplines**. Describe some personal disciplines in preparing to direct a play for the theater. List five pre-production actions that have spiritual repercussions you think are essential for the director before rehearsals start and that you have exercised.

   - **Research**. Answer the following questions:

     a. What areas of artistic experience outside of theater really interest you? Is it music, dance, movies, painting, sculpture, poetry, novels, or what? How do you think this interest can contribute to your work as a theater director?

     b. What areas outside of the direct arts experience also have captured your time and attention? What have you learned about human nature from your preoccupation with these pursuits? It might be hiking, pets, sports, or some sort of ministry work. Perhaps it's chess or games of logic or a preoccupation with the Fall of the Roman Empire.

- **Character Sources**. Take a character from history, someone like Edgar Allen Poe, George Floyd, Judas, Pilate, Søren Kierkegaard, or C.S. Lewis. Research them and discover five things that you think would be important to include in a stage production. In essence, what you are doing is finding the dramatic in people, places, or things. And then you are distilling this to make a story. You are developing an eye for the dramatic. The actual work of a director is not dissimilar to that of a playwright. Can you do the same with a place? – an abortion clinic, a school classroom, a locker room? What about a thing, a prop? —a pregnancy testing unit, an almost empty bottle of scotch, a broken cross. What you are doing is applying your dramatic imagination to the beginning of story.

- **What Do You Want to Say?** Make a list of three things that you are passionate about. Anything from abortion to cell phones to bullying to your minister's sermons, to Black Lives Matter. Then imagine a moment in time and space that involves one single event or moment of these preoccupations and relate what it looks like, where it is, what objects are present, and what happens, and why it is important? Stage this moment if in a class situation. Discuss.

2. **Authority:** We have all been in a position when we want someone to *do* something, either for us, for them, or for a cause. And we have met obstacles.

   - **Get Moving**. Describe some stratagems that you might have used to get them moving. Directing is all about telling a story through action, through objectives and obstacles. A good place to start is with those closest to you. Or you can make up a situation.

   - **Motivation**. Create a situation between two characters in which one desperately wants the other to do something. The conflict is that this character does not want to do what is being suggested. Using actors, classmates, or friends, describe the situation, the wants, and be prepared to provide the needy character with different strategies to accomplish their goal based on what you see them doing in an improvisation. Discuss afterwards what seemed to work best and why? When did the attempt fall flat on its face, and why?'

3. **Temptation:** Equipping oneself with Scripture to counter moments of temptation, both personal and in terms of the playscript that you are working with is an on-going discipline.

   - **Temptations.** Note some of the temptations that you have encountered in everything from the play selection, through audition, and into rehearsal period in working in the theater. What did you learn from this as far as personal discipline is concerned?

   - **Finding the Moral Center.** Every play has some sort of moral base to it. Characters often must make moral decisions. Using a play that you are working on or one of your favorites look up verses from Scripture that would apply to the moral conflict that is at the heart of the drama. *The Crucible* (1953), for example, examines the concept of justice and false accusation. What verses from Scripture could apply to the text and be used to communicate to actors?

4. **On the Calling:** A calling is a personal encounter, in some form or another, with a God that often turns you around in terms of the direction you are going with your art. Perhaps one's calling further defines what you believe and what you create in a more God-oriented direction.

   - **On Being Called.** Do you feel you have been called to be an artist in terms of looking to the Lord for leadership and inspiration in the creative work that you endeavor to accomplish? How has this manifested itself? What attacks do you believe you have been under from the enemy because of pursuing this calling? In other words, what has the cost been? What joy have you experienced also? What's your story here?

   - **Calling in Action.** Provide some examples from your creative work in which you feel you have realized or struggled with the idea of attempting to realize your calling. It might be anything from the selection of a play to produce, something you have written, or something you have refused to get involved in.

5. **The Proof Is in the Pudding:** Sculpting moments of significance with the actor and props is one of the joys of directing. These moments are not always indicated in the text. When you find these moments, or when you create them yourself, and you have

determined that they speak the truth in an artistic and even transcendent way, lovingly mold them.

- **Truth in Composition**. Using actors and props, find two or three moments in a play text that demonstrate what you feel is gestural truth in a moment. How do these moments create meaningful beauty and transcendent meaning? How do touch, focus, and the props function to enable and communicate this moment? See if you can find the 'image' for them in a tableaux moment.

- **Pass the Prop**. In your playscript imagine two or three moments when a prop is passed from one character to another. These are special moments because they tell the story of the relationships and the plot in super charged ways. Using two class members pass the prop using no more than one or two lines. Do it different ways and notice how important and effective good prop manipulation can be between characters.

6. **The Cost of Following Jesus**: I have found directing to be exhilarating and at the same time a truly stressful occupation. It literally takes a few weeks to wind down after a production has been mounted. It may be filled with rewards, but it is no easy task.

- **Taking Up Your Artistic Cross**. What does it mean to you to take up your cross in the Christian walk? How does this understanding transfer over into your experiences as a director? Where have you found the challenges of directing to be almost overwhelming, and how has our Lord helped to get you through?

- **Gathering Verses**. Begin gathering verses that can help you address spiritually the stresses involved with directing. One of my favorites is: "Peace I leave with you; my peace I give you. I do not give to you as the world gives. Do not let your hearts be troubled and do not be afraid" (John 14:27, NIV). What can you add to this?

Chapter 2

Theatrical Conventions

I THINK IT IS VERY IMPORTANT for the Christian director to envision an approach to theater that goes beyond the realism that is so prevalent in church sketches and sitcoms on television, and to have one's imagination engage in forms and moments that transcend this ordinary world. Why is that? Because as spiritual beings we live in two worlds at once: the phenomenal and the ordinary. So if we believe in this dual reality then finding subtle and meaningful ways of expressing this should be foundational to the full expression of our art. This does not mean that you should make Eugene O'Neill's *Long Day's Journey into Night* (1956) into an expressionistic piece. But it does mean that you should be on the look-out for scripts that are open to this kind of interpretation. I believe that a place to start this process is in understanding the idea of how to create theater conventions. I sincerely believe that if the director can grasp the concept of theater conventions, he is well on his way to mastering the particular and unique aspects that define the genre of drama. The following provides an example of what I am suggesting by looking at how to stage the idea of transcendence through an examination of the use of theater conventions.

The final page of Lucia Frangione's playscript *Espresso* (2004) reads as follows:

> ROSA: Where is Dad now? Tony? Perhaps the next life will be a better life and that is something still to hope for. It's all we're going to get. It is such an immense mystery. How can I believe that my spirit and all my good might separate from my bad when my body dies, like oil separates from water and rises into eternity?
>
> AMANTE: *The winter is past; the rains are over and gone; the season of singing has come.*
>
> ROSA: Nonna and I go to Israel in the spring, the last spring we have together before she dies. We see Bethlehem. We walk the road of Golgotha. And we float in the dead sea.

(AMANTE buoys her up and lifts her, she gasps with the rush of it
and outstretches her arms as eagles are heard above.)

THE END.[1]

The above represents a scene which captures effectively different convention modalities. It combines lyrical language and realistic language in
a non-realistic physical epiphany. It uses accompanying sound that recalls
that stirring passage from Isaiah 40:30, "they shall mount up with wings like
eagles" (NKJV). It has a male actor playing the Christ figure but not dressed
as an angel or a biblical character. It has an action signifying flying with one
actor/character carrying another. So what is meant by conventions? These
are the rules of reality established by the playwright that are introduced
early in the drama and which often have to do with non-realistic depictions
of time and space. In *Espresso*, for example, the use of two actors playing
multiple characters, including spiritual or Christ-like representations, is
established from the play's onset. It is my belief that the creative choices
which characterize the final scene from *Espresso*, a transcendent moment
realized using theatrical conventions, is an aspect of playmaking that is too
often neglected as part of the creative vocabulary of contemporary Christian dramatists and directors.

Why is this? In a broad sense it could be blamed on the evangelical
dispensational view which questions any art depiction that cannot be explained or found expressed in the Word itself. We want to be shown everything, have everything explained, and not be challenged by mystery. Thus,
we question dance as an abstraction, and perhaps shy away from truly engaging the book of Revelation. Additionally, we have been weaned on the
sitcom parameters we see on television and fail to understand the potent
use of space and time that theatrical conventions and subject matter can
present. Time and space manipulation on television and in films is usually
utilitarian. It is a means of transitioning from one real space to another,
from one time reality to another, and is accomplished technically in the
editing suite. On the stage, however, the way in which space and time is
manipulated often has a symbolic or referential quality to it. This is due
to the live nature of theater and the establishment of the illusion of time,
place, and action in a neutral space. It is seen happening before our eyes as
a conscious manipulation. And the nature of this reality is different than
the rapid juggling of images and locations that characterize the television
and film media.

The way time and space are manipulated on the stage is what we term theatrical conventions. Pseudolus sings to and addresses his audience in *A Funny Thing Happened on the Way to the Forum* (1962). He has broken the illusion of a separate time and space between audience and play. He is talking to us. But this comic intimacy is lost when Zero Mostel in the film version talks to the camera. A mime artist walks out on a blank stage, stretches out his hand, senses rain, puts up an imaginary umbrella, and shuffles off stage. If the same actions were performed on location in a film shoot the effect would be ridiculous, an obvious parody or mere recording of a theatrical convention.

These conventions are more than just tools to transform space and time. Because they are representative of a greater reality, they often become symbolic of the state of mind of the characters. I return to Frangione's *Espresso*. The actress playing Rosa takes on the roles of several of Rosa's female relatives. This is more than just a display of theatrical virtuosity. The character of Rosa is haunted by these other characters, at times obsessed with them. They are a part of her, so the convention of being transformed into multiple characters becomes a psychologically meaningful ploy.

For the theater to flourish I believe that the renewed imagination of the playwright and director must be used to create drama that engages the contemporary angst of our culture in a manner that is unique to theater. I am talking here of drama that encompasses the potent reality that we live in a moral universe, that we are capable of transcendence, and that we are not bound by material reality (which is the realm of film). Part of this challenge is how to create a valid, meaningful, and aesthetically moving depiction of humans as spiritual beings in the physical world. To understand how theater can articulate humankind's encounter with the more-than-material-reality, it is first necessary to understand the basic nature of the theatrical in theater.

The Nature of the Theatrical

Theater is artifice and it should not pretend to be something that it is not. Its main ambitions should not be to try to convince us that somehow, we are being transported into a realistic world that mirrors our daily experience. Theater is artificial. What our physical senses make of what is around us is hardly the sum of who we are as human beings in this universe. The Greeks, William Shakespeare, and later the symbolists and expressionists at the turn of the last century all consider a fuller universe than merely the physical. Dense poetic language is used. Masks prevail in Greek and Roman drama. Shakespeare and the Greeks put gods on the stage, and ghosts, magic, monologues, and direct address to the audience are often used conventions. Changes in location and time are articulated using a table, a sound, or a prop.

Through the inclusion of the mystery of the unseen, theater becomes true metaphysical play. By expanding the boundaries of reality, we ask the audience to expand their boundaries and stretch their imagination. More rather than less becomes possible using challenging theatrical conventions. The basic tenants of our belief system, which holds that we live in a universe sustained by an all knowing, all loving God, is the starting point for denying an exclusively materialistic outlook on life and art. The theater I am prescribing is one that, through positing the possibility of multi-levels of reality, explores what we are as human beings in this cosmos. In realistic theater we can talk about ourselves as spiritual beings. In the theater of artifice and radical conventions, we can physically express through movement and sound a hint to the otherness of the spiritual world that surrounds us.

Genesis 1:27 tells us that we are made in the image of God. Thus, God is an image maker; and if we are made in his image then we also are image makers. We are designed to create metaphors. God made us metaphor-makers because he wants to provide us with a means to approach the mystery of his existence. This ability is what defines our humanity. It is the Creative Mandate.

The more realistic or static our artwork becomes the more the scope of our image making is dulled or reduced and is less challenging to our imaginations. In theater we should not attempt to hide the rules of our pretend game, but should instead celebrate that the source of our reality is the live presence of the actor, the live presence of the audience, and the knowledge that truth can be contained in artifice. In other words, at the same time we know the actor in his imaginary work is a liar, we simultaneously acknowledge that he can speak and act great truth. Theater can only continue to uniquely exist if these elements of artifice are praised, not looked upon as shortcomings. In this way, as we celebrate reality in all its fullness, we can attempt to make the transcendent a concrete artistic reality on the stage without losing its mystery through literalization or cheap special effects.

I am all for using *a vista* scene changes, in which the audience sees exactly what is going on during the scene change, unlike the magical scene transitions so often glimpsed on the musical Broadway stage. For example, in a production of my play *Five Cups of Coffee* (2006), which premiered at the Lamb's Players Theater in San Diego, the gates at the garden of Eden were moved off-stage while the action was still going on.

What can be and often are problematic from an aesthetic standpoint are the attempts by Christian creative artists to depict aspects of spiritual reality on the stage. To communicate a sense of the transcendent spiritual reality often involves the use of concrete theatrical conventions. The way in which this is articulated on the stage can be sappy, condescending, and predictable. On the other hand, it can also be provocative, challenging, and mysterious.

In her essays compiled in *Mystery and Manners*, American author and believer Flannery O'Conner suggests that to make the supernatural real we must first make the natural world supercharged with significant reality. She discusses finding the moment of grace which is often expressed in a gesture that is completely within character, but beyond character, organic to the moment and yet wholly unexpected, and so creating a moment that touches mystery. O'Connor borrows from theology the idea of an image that speaks on multiple levels, and she is particularly interested in attempting to express what she terms the "anagogical level" or that which expresses the Divine life and our participation in it through the temporal rather than the spiritual.[2]

To realize this form of theatrical transcendence will require an intimate knowledge of human character and the often inarticulate and varied attempts that humans use to reach for the inexpressible. It will need conventions that will be able to abstract human thought and action without losing their wellspring in the immediately physical, which would almost seem to be a definition of theater itself. The director is challenged to know how imagery works, the archetypal challenges it poses, and how to project it through prop, gesture, light, movement, and sound so that the sense of the transcendent can resonate within the audience.

So we return to the final image with which we began this discussion, from the play *Espresso* (2004). Rosa is lifted up by a spiritual being. But this being is an actor. And the Christ figure/actor sweats. He is not wearing wings or carrying a harp. She circles the stage on his back; she does not fly off, but she is transported. And so are we.

Discussion Questions and Exercises

1. **Making the Abstract Concrete**. Take some examples from Psalms and experiment with creating this dual reality that is referred to in this section. The language is suggestive, and the challenge is to find a movement, sound, prop, even dialogue equivalency in your creative imagination that might ground these lines or moments in something tangible.

   - For example, take Psalm 1:1: "Happy are those who do not follow the advice of the wicked, or take the path that sinners tread, or sit in the seat of scoffers" (NRSV).

     Here you might have a sturdy chair and have an actor approach it, serpent like, caressing it, scoffing at everything in the room that they think might be noble or virtuous. Then climb over the chair, slowly ripping a Bible to shreds, even chewing on pages. Don't only occupy and sit, but take over the chair physically, lewdly, peremptorily. This is their throne of mockery.

   - In another example, consider Psalm 1:3: "They are like trees planted by streams of water, which yield their fruit in its season, and their leaves do not wither. In all that they do, they prosper" (NRSV). Three actors moving as one "swim" in concert, touching, reveling, their "fruit" is a song, a caress, musical laughter, innocence enjoyed, growing together as in a vine that twists toward the sun. Perhaps one becomes pregnant, and this is celebrated.

   - You have an entire Bible to draw from. Be sure to read Isaiah, who provides some of the most lyrical moments in Scripture along with The Song of Solomon, Lamentations, Revelation.

2. **Finding the "Other" in Plays**. The Greeks, Shakespeare, and expressionistic playwrights such as August Strindberg, Georg Kaiser, and Guillaume Apollinaire as well as Eugene O'Neill and the "theater of the absurd" dramatists explore the extra-real in their dramas. In the Greeks, gods were appearing onstage in everything from Aeschylus' *The Orestian Trilogy* (458 BC) to Sophocles' cruel jokester Athena in *Ajax* (442 BC), to Pentheus being persuaded to dress as a woman by Dionysus in Euripides' *The Bacchae* (405 BC). All are supported by a Chorus that dances and chants. Shakespeare wrote

in iambic pentameter, crafting monologues with direct audience address and including all sorts of ghosts, imaginative heaths for King Lear, gods flying in on chariots, and ending with Prospero's displays of magic in Shakespeare's *The Tempest* (c. 1611).

- What moments can you find or imagine in the great classical and contemporary playwrights that go beyond realism in depicting a broader scope of human behavior and dreams, in another reality? Describe, show pictures, and discuss. How would you see these being represented on the stage? What productions have you seen that have grafted more abstract images into realistic plays?

Chapter 3

Imagery

IMAGERY CAN BE CLASSIFIED WITH PLOT AND CHARACTER as a significant element in the art of telling a story. All language is imagery. When we say the word "red" it represents the image for the color in our minds. Each of us will imagine red in a different context as it engages our memory, backstory, and immediate environmental situations, and though the color might change in hue, "redness" is the common descriptive denominator for each person. The same with the written word. The letters r-e-d say something specific to our imaginations. The letters stand for the color. The emphasis in the definition of imagery as representative of sensory experience also ties it resolutely to the creative fields of writing, acting, and directing. Writers "move" their audiences emotionally through the truth of sensory imagery. King Lear's depiction of the stormy heath as an image of nature gone wild and as an image of the mangled state of his mind are what give that scene its visual resilience. Directors use metaphor to suggest a movement or an interpretation to an actor. How often is the director required to use such phrases as "It's like. . ." or "Think of this as if. . ." as a verbal tool to get through to the actor's sensibilities. And then there is the on-going truth that the actor's gestural life is an imagistic presentation that suggests the truth of a moment in visual terms. The actor portraying a role is a walking, talking visual metaphor.

I think we create images because we innately sense that there is a world or dimension beyond our own that can somehow be captured when wedded with the image-making capabilities of our imaginations. Creating images is a way of collaborating with other people's imaginations and with the multi-dimensionality of the Universe itself. We order the stars into constellations and make stories out of the pictures by which we imagine and remember the movements of the heavens.

The oldest pictures found on the walls of ancient caves are representations of nature, an attempt to capture some sort of reality that we experience daily. They represent a cry saying, "I was here." In other words, we establish a sense of identity through creating imagery. We try to explain the mysteries we do not understand by creating imagery. We try to own reality in some way through depicting it. Interestingly, some of the early bison drawings depict the animals with more than four legs to capture their motion. The art on the cave walls is art in action.

Imagery is at the basis of all ritual. In early rites the Shaman or priest would dress up in a buffalo skin and dance to the accompaniment of drums and shaking devices, repeating phrases, and seeking to communicate with the gods to make the next hunt a successful one. The Shaman might carry a talisman, which is supposed to be endowed with special powers. Thus, we see in the use of props, costumes, dance, music, and song a conglomeration of image making that tries to influence our destiny by getting us on the good side of the gods.

The impulse to create images may also stem from our having to contend with our ultimate destiny—physical death. Imagery manifests itself as an urge to immortalize ourselves through painting, poetry, sculpture, and architecture. It is an attempt to return to the pre-Fall state where we were one with him and beyond death. Andre Bazin, the famous French critic and film theorist, has noted in *What is Cinema,* that it is through the imagery used in story that we create mini-destinies that we hope will ensure that at least some aspect of our creative being will live on in the audience's memory.[1]

Because we are gifted with the five senses, especially with that of sight, we are inundated with images on a second-by-second basis as we experience life. Even in our dreams we "see" through the mind's eye, creating representative stories, moments, and events that are manufactured by our unconscious minds. Our memory is a kaleidoscope of images, being a virtual storehouse of picture after picture of where we have been, whom we have seen, and even who we are. A distant whistle takes us back to lying in bed in childhood listening to a scheduled train whiz by.

Our memories are not static. We adapt them to compensate and to adjust so we can experience less suffering, angst, or loss, or to build up and bolster our images of ourselves. Harold Pinter's plays are noted for using altered memory as an aggressive tool for threatening the identity of others and protecting our own fragile facades. Without any conscious planning or structuring, our image retention, or what we choose to remember or see or even think about, reflects an aspect of who we are, of how we see the world, and of what we are running away from or toward. Memories tell the story of what we fear or desire through pictures and actions.

I believe that our love of stories has its roots in our attempts to organize, utilize, concentrate, and control the images that surround us. I would suggest that the form or image-making process is an essential ingredient of our humanness as we strive to better understand and control the formless nature of our feelings.

How often have we as parents been asked to go over a picture book one more time as we put our children to bed? Picture books begin the progress to the predominance of the written word. The child is hearing the written word and associating it with a picture or with several pictures. Since the child cannot read yet, this is a process in which she is understanding the word in terms of a separate picture. The on-going popularity of comic books, illustrated books, and of course, the rich and varied world of film and television, is explained by their provision of a moving tapestry of conjoining script with picture, or with taking the written word and finding equivalences for it. This is at the heart of our communicative process as human beings.

As children progress in their development, they begin to be able to take the written word, without the picture, and form a picture of their own of what the word means to them. For example, the word "bed" brings up images of one's own bed; or a bed seen before; or of a combination of different beds experienced; or of a bed that is archetypal "bed-ness." Unlike Plato, I am not sure that "bed-ness" is an actual archetype that exists in heaven as a true metaphysical reality.

The director will often select a script for production that has identifiable imagery depictions throughout it, or at least has the potential for this kind of development. It is part of his artistic vision not only to realize these patterns, but also to bring her own image building sensibility in bringing the images to life on the stage. Hopefully, the writer should be aware of the effective use of vivid descriptive moments in the story development that provide material for the director to recognize, appreciate, and hopefully realize in her interpretation of the story for a live audience. If not, the director should be challenged by creating image systems from her unique imagination that will help to carry the story.

I believe that the conscious structuring of creative image systems, symbols, and metaphors that reflect the dynamic movement of the story through environment, character, and action is a process that moves the play into a realm of deeper meaning, a realm which could be considered an evolutionary aspect of our humanness, and a realm which challenges and enlightens who we are as human beings. And I think this process is God-ordained. He wants us to be making these connections between concentrated imagery and story because that is one of the ways that he has revealed himself to us in his Word.

To elaborate further, an image system is the concentrated and varied depiction of symbols, images, and metaphors in an artfully focused and progressive manner. Water imagery could be expressed in water, ice, snow, rain, tears, sprinklers, showers, and so forth. The image system becomes effective to the degree that the use of it is progressively more complicated and enhances and even tells the story and reflects the character arc that is being portrayed.

Wind imagery can reflect natural actions in a film, such as a hurricane with its raging winds. Then there is tangential wind imagery: a character in the same film who carries a mini fan around with her, always seeking out a breeze to subdue her temper and her being overweight. Perhaps such a character huffs and puffs, as if there is a storm within wanting to get out. In this instance the character has internalized the image of wind/storm.

In addition, wind imagery can exhibit more varied traits, i.e., a woman catches the breeze on a warm summer night and it gently and seductively blows her hair back. This is a subjective use of the wind imagery, meaning that the wind relates to each character according to the character's attributes. Or just the opposite. A particularly neat and orderly character is annoyed and tested by the bothersome wind that keeps disrupting his orderly existence. We sense the personified use of the idea of wind.

The natural elements can and often do reflect the psychological and plot positioning of a character. For example, William Shakespeare's *Hamlet* (c. 1600) could be playing madness in a hall of mirrors. Usually there is a thematic relevance behind the use of imagery. For instance, a person's life has gone to hell and there is a storm outside. Things are rotten in Denmark because of the murder of a King; therefore, this rottenness infects the lives, actions, and places that the hero travels. There are numerous ways of expressing imagery as an artistic and even a narrative tool in the director's toolbox.

Another kind of image system is that of anchoring images, which applies the judicious use of props. An example would be *Hedda Gabler* (1891) opening her father's pistols early in the play; shooting at Judge Brack as he moves through the garden; passing the pistol off to Lovborg, and finally committing suicide with one of these firearms at the very end of the play. These pistols stand for the masculine imagery that Hedda has surrounded herself with and her attempts to emulate her late father, General Gabler, a dominating controller and emasculator of men.

Another notable use of imagery can be found in the all-important concluding image, which is tied directly to the thematic discovery at the end of the story. Examples would be the burning of Citizen Kane's childhood sled entitled Rosebud in the sweeping panorama of workers burning the wealthy man's lifetime collections and symbolizing the loss of his childhood. In C. P. Taylor's *Good* (1989) the "good" Professor Halder ends standing in a Nazi uniform at Auschwitz as he decides who will live and die, an icon of brutality and ethnic cleansing. The students in John Keating's prep school English classroom stand on their desks in tribute to their fired lecturer, an image repeated throughout *Dead Poet's Society* (1992), and one which represents their defiant loyalty. As a director, what is the image that you want emblazoned on the minds of the audience and that speaks the final truth of the production you have mounted?

Image clustering is a system of image analysis by North American literary theorist and critic Kenneth Burke, which clusters like image systems within circles. These circles are then labeled. To the degree that the circles overlap connotes the strength and emphasis of the most dominant image systems.[2] For example, in Shakespeare's *A Midsummer Night's Dream* (c. 1596) there is flower, drug, and sleep imagery. The flowers are used as the source of the drugs and therefore the two circles or systems of imagery overlap.

Through using this method, one can discover the meanings that key symbols and words have for the writer, or rhetor. Burke explains the central idea of cluster analysis in which every writer (rhetor) contains a set of implicit equations. He uses the term "associational clusters." And you may, by examining his work, find "what goes with what" in these clusters—what kinds of acts, images, personalities, and situations go with his notions of heroism, villainy, consolation, despair, and other archetypal concepts.[3]

In Scripture, imagery is a tool which is used throughout to depict the various levels of interpretation that provide such a rich tapestry of meaning, not only for our knowledge of the narrative, but also for how we *see* and perhaps *feel* the story unfold. The Good Shepherd, the sacrificial lamb, the blood on lintels during Passover, seeds, weddings, water, light, and darkness, to mention just a few, are provided so that we cannot only imagine the moment, but see it realized throughout time, space, and action to have universal significance. It also serves as another way of reflecting, through God-ordained patterns and motifs, the mystery and the interconnectedness of his creative vision. Think of how he uses the image of blood. Cain's murder contaminates the earth with the shed blood of Abel. The

Abrahamic Covenant is realized through blood sacrifice. Blood saves the believer through the sacrifice of the lamb at Passover. Blood sacrifice rituals established in the Law help to redeem Cain's original curse, if only momentarily. God redeems mankind from his sins through the shed blood on the cross by the Lamb of God. And this is merely a cursory look at the image of blood imagery in Scripture.

It is fitting for the director to become a student of image systems and their significance. It is a tool that he will use repeatedly. Imagery is another way of telling the story. It undergirds the theme and provides a context that can be realized throughout the developing action of a production. Some tools on how to discover and create these important image constructs for the stage can be seen in the following chapter.

Discussion Questions and Exercises

1. **Imagery in Action**. Using an actor or actors provide a simple action such as "cross to the table from your sitting position." Have prepared or improvise using imagistic language in the form of metaphors to describe the cross. An example might be: "Move to the table as if you were saying goodbye to it and all it stood for in your life." Watch which of your metaphorical suggestions seems to be most effective and discuss why.

2. **Identify and Construct Imagery in a Text**. Select a play that is rich in imagery and select a play that is seemingly devoid of imagistic content. In the former identify the various image systems, and how they work and amplify the meaning and visual context of the play. I recommend using Shakespeare, the Greeks, or plays that go beyond immediate realism. In the latter, perhaps in a more realistic comedy or farce, identify what images exist, But also add imagery contexts that you feel might be relevant. For example: I saw a production of Ibsen's realistic domestic drama *The Doll's House* (1879), in which the interior set constituted a room filled with chairs, and as the play progressed and Nora became closer and closer to leaving, the chairs were carried offstage. The final image had the walls of the house fly out leaving a huge, sculptured image of a pile of chairs reaching up perhaps fourteen feet and symbolizing all the middle class and repressive trappings from which Nora had escaped.

3. **The Culminating Image**. Select three plays that you have an affinity for. Describe the final image that you feel is projected by the author as the curtain goes down. How would you stage this moment so that its visual identity and meaning would be emblazoned on the audience's mind in terms of culminating significance? In Chapter 2, the elevated image of the character being carried about the stage in *Espresso* (2004) captures this reality. I had the final image of my production of Shakespeare's *Much Ado about Nothing* (1623) with Feste the Clown sprouting wings and flying off the island as a result of the mindless lovemaking causing him to vacate the sentimental 'happy ending' premises. What can you come up with?

4. **Biblical Imagery**. In the *Dictionary of Biblical Imagery* (1998) there is an exhaustive catalogue of imagery context as represented in Scripture.[4] Can you find other biblical image systems besides the reference to "blood" in the text that might influence a production you could conceive of and which functions as a story element? What are the associational images? How do they work? How can they be made concrete?

Chapter 4

The Director and the
Central Image Concept

ONE OF THE PRIMARY CONTRIBUTIONS that the director makes to the creative process is the development of a *central image concept*. This is a pervasive image, with its organic roots in the playscript, around which the director frames or shapes his production concept. The costuming, props, set design, acting style, and space and time interpretations should all reflect on this central image. It is an artistic aspect that is not abstract. It can be seen. For example, a director who says his concept is that of a moth fluttering around a flame for *The Rainmaker* (1954) has probably distanced himself from a visual representation that can be understood and appreciated by fellow designers and by the audience.

For an arena production of *Who's Afraid of Virginia Woolf?* (1962) at Transylvania University, director Thomas Van Brunt conceived a boxing or wrestling ring as a central concept which framed the action in such a way that the image served the interactive patterns of movement, sound, and pacing in this conflict-driven drama. No, I am not suggesting that ropes be put up, with stools and a bell ringing to suggest that a beat or scene is finished. But the characters emerge from their corners (George's library, Martha's bar) as territorial necessities, and retreat to their respective havens to regroup and re-strategize for the next round. No clanging bell, but dropped drinks, doors slamming, and other cacophonous sounds mark beat transitions. The lights are hung low over the round staging, and characters leave the playing area by walking down steps at various entrances. In the end Martha is on her knees and there is no apparent winner, as George kneels to embrace her. A kind of tag team semblance brings characters into and out of the fray in what comes close to being a life and death struggle over power, memory, and psychological dysfunction. The boxing ring image enhances the battleground conflict. The characters strip to a degree, sweaters, ties, shoes being removed as they sweat, spit, throw verbal, and at times physical, punches at each other. The appearance of civilization is stripped from their upper middle-class environs and lifestyle.

Creating a central image demands an intellectual understanding of the playscript, but it should always lead to a more intuitive and sensory-oriented layering which enhances and undergirds both the meaning and the human striving that good drama should represent. In other words, it should enhance the thematic and psychological journey of the play visually. Here are some additional examples:

In Michael Frayn's play *Copenhagen* (1998), which was based on the 1941 meeting between atomic physicists Niels Bohr and Werner Heisenberg, the director's contribution was to have the small cast of characters circle each other and interact in terms of atomic elements. As they jockeyed for understanding and revelation, the comings together and separations were played out subtly through these movement patterns resulting in a sense of destiny that the future held something ominous that was being formed here.

In a production I directed of *Story Theater* (1971), a delightful conglomeration of Grimm's fairy tales by Paul Sills, I used the paintings of Renaissance artist Pieter Brueghel featuring town squares, peasant weddings, and children's games to capture the reckless energy of these unpredictable environments. His painting *The Battle Between Carnival and Lent* (1559) was the primary source used, as the holy bumps up against the profane, and the production mounted a *mise en scene*, or arrangement of props and set pieces, that captured this conflict with a small wooden stage and primitive curtain being the source for the masked and often darkly interpreted fairy tales.

In an original theatrical musical documentary that portrayed the turbulent history of the steel industry and its workers entitled *Steel/City* (1976), the set was constructed entirely from steel scaffolding, going three stories high, with most of the props being the actual artifacts used in the process of making steel, especially in the decades spanning 1880–1920. The image created and hopefully communicated was the mill as the ultimate reality for the suffering and triumphs of a migrant influx into Pittsburgh during these years. There was no escaping the overbearing presence of the mills, which were built from and produced iron and steel made of earth, fire, water, and air. The human figure endured but was also dwarfed by this elemental gorging process. The image was of a monolith that consumed and at the same time gave mythic significance to the people who survived it.

I directed a production at the University of Pittsburgh of *Marry-Go-Wrong* (1880), a farce by French playwright Georges Feydeau that captured the brash escapades of these comically put-upon characters through an image of pulling taffy. That is right—the central image was a movement motif. Set in a valentine decorated box analogous to the most prettified candy offering, the nineteenth-century characters tugged and scraped their way to a comic frenzy, with the visual physical extensions finally overflowing the stage into the audience, all ending in a pile of total exhaustion with an array of costume pieces and accessories strewn across the stage like discarded candy wrappers.

In directing Harold Pinter's *Old Times* (1971) and identifying the main action as being a psychological mind game pitting the past against the present, the set I envisioned was a platform that seemed to be floating just off the ground with a minimalistic selection of modern furniture. The ties to reality were tenuous at best in this beige, shag-rugged platform that seemed to be suspended inches from the floor. It had the feeling of a dream gone slightly awry.

In directing Christopher Marlowe's *Doctor Faustus* (1592), I created a design set in a 1930s dark carnival located in a dusty Mid-west town during Depression times. Marlowe's extreme characterizations, demons, and gross comic scenes of dismemberment and hangings lent a morbid "grand guignol" feeling to the Professor's hell-bent journey, a feeling so named for the famous French theater that specialized in horror shows.

In a production of William Shakespeare's *A Midsummer Night's Dream* (c. 1596), I found dramatic equivalences to Japanese Anime/Manga images, with characters zooming from place to place, large-eyed, wild colorful spiked wigs, a plethora of fake flowers, and of course, martial arts. It was a cartoon free-for-all that caught the magic and blink of an eye movement which characterizes Shakespeare's classic comic dream-like romp.

David Storey's *The Contractor* (1969) features a three-act drama in which in the first act workers erect a wedding tent on stage. Act Two features aspects of the wedding reception, and Act Three depicts the taking down of the tent. The play provides a vivid contrast between the working class and upper middle class in a realistic setting which supports the theme that this could be all of our lives: we all set up our tent, our house, our memories in an empty field which ends up being taken down and deserted. A pessimistic message to be sure, but the gritty energy of the workers is palpable and lingers as a kind of echo to Sisyphus, the Greek figure who received eternal punishment after trying to cheat death. The important thing here is that the central image is constructed and torn down, and in such a way that the activity has a special meaning about existence itself.

The creation of the central image is perhaps the most essential creative tool that the director brings to a production but can also be misplaced and misdirected. A production of French playwright Moliere's *Scapin the Schemer* (1671) placed the dramatic farcical action as a kind of baseball game with characters sliding into bases and hitting or striking out on comic routines. The production was mindless and left the audience wondering what the original must have looked like. A staging of *Julius Caesar* (1599) in Central Park in 2017 tried to recreate the assassination of President Kennedy, with Brutus becoming a kind of Vice President Lyndon B. Johnson and with Cassius as a black militant, which kept the audience constantly trying to figure out the rationalizations for the modern equivalences.

The forced development of the central image can be the downfall of the director's production. This usually involves an attempt to communicate visually and often at the expense of the play some producer or director's personal agenda. The purposeful breaking of the intended genre of the play, such as turning a murder thriller into a comic romp, or a farce into realistic angst, is an abuse of power and good taste by the director. David Garrick in the eighteenth century was known for his happy endings to Shakespeare's tragedies *Romeo and Juliet* (1597) and *King Lear* (c. 1606) to appease the emerging middle class in London. A commercial choice but thematically questionable.

The central image concept that you have developed is the primary directive that you provide for your stage designer. For *Doctor Faustus* (1592), I inundated my designer with pictures of entertainment wagons, carnivals, masks, and 1930s Depression-era landscapes. He worked out the details, but the imagery patterns originated in my imagination. *Hedda Gabler* (1891) featured huge, windowed doors with sweeping curtains that Hedda's long royal dresses mirrored; and which helped establish a sensuous throne room peopled with a harem of men that she sought to control. The low-ceilinged Scandinavian household was replaced with almost gothic hugeness as she ruled her man-centered court.

And Sarah Laughed (2006), the biblical story of Abraham, featured three Sarah's, each a different aspect of the biblical original, and was set as a stand-up comedy routine that explored the journey together in terms of different kinds of laughter and song. The set had several tables placed on the in-the-round stage floor where customers chatted and ate and drank appetizers as the show went on around them. Abe appeared as a statuesque figure sitting upstage in a rocker.

You have some personal connection with the work you have chosen to direct that is yours, not necessarily your designers, so you are obligated as an artist to communicate your vision as effectively as possible to your design staff. A unified central image concept is the place to start in accomplishing this. I do admit that some productions lend themselves to this sort of imaginative task better than others. *The Odd Couple* (1965) with its messy apartment is just that, a messy apartment. It is hard to improve on Thornton Wilder's descriptions of the minimalistic leanings of *Our Town* (1938) with its fragmented scenery and symbolic use of step ladders, or Peter Terson's *Zigger-Zagger* (1967) which is comprised of a composition of bleachers that face the audience and represent the backdrop of a soccer crazed world that takes place on the empty downstage area.

The central image concept has extensive scope and importance. It can appear as movement motifs and in the use of artistic and cultural paradigms or overlays such as Brueghel-inspired carnivals, sports motifs, the circus, cabarets, and the use of other time periods such as putting Shakespeare in more contemporary periods. It often establishes the set as a personified character that changes organically during the process of the play. It can also feature a natural phenomenon such as a drought, a plague, a storm, or other event as an overriding image. And it often is used effectively to reflect varied states of mind and philosophical bents (such as expressionism or existentialist "theater of the absurd"). It enhances and supports the inherent theme of the play, provides visual depth and context, and remains the director's most important contribution to the artistic unity of a production.

God filled us with the gift of image making. It is an honored privilege. As we view the dominant culture around us we see too often how this gift has been compromised in the celebration of the dark side and in the expression of just bad art. It is part of our obligation to use our gifts to counter these influences, and to explore and find ways of expressing God's love and light through our image-making. No easy task, but a worthy one to pursue.

Discussion Questions and Exercises

1. **Finding Your Central Image.** Using one of your favorite plays, determine a central image concept and articulate why you have chosen this imagery in terms of unity concerning theme, action motifs, period or time classification, costuming, lighting, set design,

and significant props. Also be able to express your overall central image in a brief sentence or two.

2. **Analogous Imagery.** Going to Pinterest or another photo source, look up as many different set design concepts for a play of your choice, and then guess what the production's central image concept might be. How do they differ? What are the deciding aesthetic factors that point you toward making your conclusions? A good one to practice on is Eugene O'Neill's *Desire Under the Elms* (1924). Try this also with Shakespeare and Greek drama where the differences would be most striking.

3. **Central Image Research.** Using a play of your choice, gather research material that would support your central image concept. For example: you are setting *The Tempest* (c. 1611) on an island in the Philippines. Your research should include materials that a hut might be built out of; pictures of the scenic landscape; tropical sound effects; bamboo structures; primitive hats and other loose native clothing; shipwreck refuse; pictures of native monster figures (Caliban) and other mythical creatures (Ariel). What period do you want to put it in? What does magic mean to you? How is it presented? Are you on the beach or inland? What period are the shipwreck characters? And so on.

Chapter 5

Script Analysis

THE DIRECTOR NEEDS TO DEVELOP an awareness and sensitivity to the dramatic, structural, thematic and characterization elements that comprise a well written script. If she is not sensitive or aware of beats, the given circumstances, discovering the character arcs, how plot points function, subtext, and imagery the result will be an incomplete understanding of the play and failure in communicating its meaning.

Kinds of Beats

There are two kinds of *beats*: those intensifying beats that work directly to build an action, and beats that are more subtle, oftentimes revealing inner aspects of character in a contemplative sense. For example, in *Hamlet* (c. 1600) when Gertrude describes the death of Ophelia her speech is a single mood beat; or Willy Loman's entrance at the top of *Death of a Salesman* (1949) when he first comes on stage late at night, confused, distracted, broken. The number of varied beats in this opening sequence reflects the state of mind of poor Willie.

It should be noted that in mood beats you never ask an actor to try to play a mood. Actors play actions, they are always doing. So when Gertrude comes on in *Hamlet*, she might be in shock, she might still be overwhelmed by the images that she saw, she might be wet and out of breath from fishing Ophelia out of the water, but what is she doing? She could be doing several things: her speech is a cry for help to Claudius because she realizes that she has also had thoughts of suicide. She wants to get herself cleaned up, purged of the dirt from outside and the dirt from within. She wants to make Claudius see the wreckage he has wrought, and so forth. You do not play moods; you play actions.

Beats and the Director

The director's work with beats begins before the rehearsal process begins. He divides the script up into beats, labeling each beat with an action verb which sums up the motivation for the character who dominates the beat. Two things here: locating the beats and identifying who is driving the beat. In other words, whose beat is it?

If, for example, during an argument a father starts off by trying to find out why his son is taking drugs, but the son turns the table and attacks his father successfully for his alcoholic tendencies, bringing him to tears, the dominant character has changed so usually the direction and intent of the beat has changed also.

If you find out that you are labeling beats using the same word, look to the script but also look to your understanding of character. Dig deeper and harder to find the shadings of meaning in changing beat strategies.

If you find that you have lots of beats on every page of your script, you have probably identified sub-beats as beats. The result will be that your production could have a choppy or overly energetic feel to it, like an engine turning over but not really engaging.

One of the problems with identifying and working with beats is that if you have two characters on stage, each probably has different wants and different actions to accomplish their objectives. In the opening of *Death of a Salesman*, for example, Willy wants to find out what went wrong out there on the road; at the same time Linda is trying to comfort Willy, to calm him down, to find out what happened out there but for different reasons. Their beat transitions will not necessarily be at the same place. So you are charting two different routes for your characters, but they are always intersecting. And one of them will be dominant over the other. Willy is more desperate than Linda, even though both characters have their own desperation. The primary beats are those which are determined by the dominant character, and the motivation for most of your movement will be instigated around the needs and wants of your dominant character.

Beats in Rehearsal

A positive aspect of a rehearsal process is to go over the script one on one with the actor talking about the beat breakdown before you start blocking. You are not blocking at this point. You are doing script work and talking about the wants of the actors' characters with them. Some directors and actors feel that this kind of textural work is not helpful, that the actors should "discover" the beats for themselves during the rehearsal process, that at no point should the director provide a beat designation for them. Certainly, the director wants the actors to have the experience of creating their own beats, and the actor's natural blocking should be a result of his awareness of where the beats are. But neither the director nor the actor can help but make some early decisions about beats before the rehearsal begins. If the director is thinking in terms of movement and blocking, then he will already be making decisions about where the beats are going to be identified. So will the actor. As they pick up the script and read it over, they cannot help but notice just where their action objectives change or are realized, and even though they might not think "beat," they are consciously beginning to think of choices they can enact to make the action happen. The important thing is that whether the director or the actor make choices before rehearsal in terms of beat identification, they must always remain flexible and be ready to change their preconceived ideas in accordance with what is happening on the stage during rehearsals. Let's say that you have done a beat breakdown prior to rehearsals, but the actor you cast has different rhythms, different strengths, and sees the character from a slightly different viewpoint. This can affect the beat distribution as you first envisioned it.

William Ball, in his book *A Sense of Direction*, lays out a process which I find to be particularly helpful, and which has been interpreted and consolidated below:

- You will rehearse a section of the play which is usually built around three or four beats.
- You will identify the beats with the actors and tell them where the scene will start and where the scene will end.
- You will run through the scene without stopping.
- You will give notes or observations and then you will tell them that "now we are going to stop and go as we progress through this beat."
- Always rehearse through a beat transition.
- Run all the beats again, without stopping, giving notes, and proceeding onto the next section of beats.[1]

The above sounds somewhat technical from a director and actor standpoint. The primary purpose of this sort of approach is to communicate with the actor the process that you are going through, when you will be stopping them, why, and when you will let them run through certain sections. Remember, it is possible for the director to have made pre-rehearsal choices insofar as beats are concerned, but in the actual process do not say to the actors, "this beat starts here and ends here." The director would like the actors to feel that they are discovering the beat for themselves. There is some risk here: as a director you must be both subtle and lovingly manipulative. You also must be aware that in the process of working out the beats with the actor that the actor's instincts might be more appropriate to the moment than yours, so be flexible and be ready to change your beat designation when necessary.

If you sense that something is wrong with a certain scene, stop and go back to doing beat transition work, making sure that you and the actor agree. If you have not worked out your beats with enough specificity during the rehearsal process it will come back to haunt you during tech week. Always find the time to stop and work beats, just giving notes will not make it happen. This goes whether you work with amateurs or professionals. Two days before I opened my production of *Cyrano de Bergerac* (1897) for the Three Rivers Shakespeare Festival in 1985, Jay Brazeau, the name actor, stopped the rehearsal during a scene where he is sitting on a table and the ensemble is running around him, swords out, by saying, "Gil, we haven't worked the beats in this scene. I'm not sure what is happening, just seems like everyone is running around." So, I stopped the run through, and we worked the scene for twenty minutes primarily breaking it down to beats in terms of motivational actions. Problem solved.

What Is a Beat Transition?

Director, remember this saying (which is usually true): an actor will always move during a beat transition. Always. One of the ways that you determine blocking is red flagging beat transitions and knowing that you must move your people during this period. It can be small, but every beat transition is characterized by some need for physical action.

During the rehearsal process, you can ask the actor what they want to do to accomplish their immediate action in this beat or that beat. The language of communication between actor and director works best at the beat level because it is the level of immediate action. It keeps the director from going off on long wordy descriptions or instructions using too much flowery language. Beat transitions demand the language of action. They are realized in the realm of the physical; they are most often the language of sensory tasks.

You can also ask the actor to play his inner monologue out loud during the beat transition. This inner monologue is what the actor as character is thinking internally at any moment in terms of executing actions on stage. In this way you can discover if the actor is thinking of his actions in specific enough and correct terms. And you might learn something from them. Remember, when externalizing the inner monologue, the actor has to be a playwright of sorts, always talking in the first person, and relating to what they see and want and how they mean to accomplish what they want in logical progression. This can also provide a measure for determining how much the actor is "in the moment" in terms of the detailed imaginative work that is required on a continuing basis. By the time the opening night rolls around hopefully your actors will have internalized these beat transitions so that they flow naturally without having to think or analyze them.

An important thing about beat transitions is that they always involve a choice or choices by the character to be realized or explored. They always involve a change in direction, rhythm, strategy, need. They almost always raise the stakes in the relationship between the dominant and subordinate characters. What if you are doing a play that does not function on motivationally built actions, such as an expressionistic or absurd piece? Beats still apply, but often they are worked out formalistically rather than motivationally.

Try having your actors first read through a sequence in which the beats are identified. In the next read through, encourage the actors to move during the beat transitions, but always in terms of seeking the fulfillment of objectives. Note with them what the beat transitions tell them about the characters. Note how this approach is a way of organically "blocking" a scene from a motivational standpoint. Then try adding a prop in a beat scene transition. Note how helpful and emblematic it can be. A prop passed meaningfully between actors tells a gestural story all by itself. (See Appendix 3, for more information on use of props.)

Literal and Essential Actions

A beat transition is characterized by the following: physical action, movement, and reactions that are usually more pronounced than other moments that are not transitions. An example of a change in objective: Ilse brings out the pistol in that pivotal scene in the film *Casablanca* (1942). She has tried pity, demanding, coyness; now it is violence. New beat transition. Try and sense the build in a scene. If the conversation takes a different turn but the character that is driving the beat does not really change his strategy, then you probably do not have a new beat.

In the book *A Practical Handbook for the Actor*, the authors define these two terms: *literal* and *essential actions*. It is helpful in every beat transition to define the changing actions in these terms.[2] What is the character literally doing? The key to answering this question is to be as literal as possible. Do not embellish what is happening on the printed page. Phrase what the character is doing in a single, precise sentence. Here is an example: A man enters a room, reaches for his pipe, searches for his tobacco pouch, takes his tobacco pouch from his desk drawer, opens the pouch, fills the pipe, and takes out his matches. What is the character literally doing? He wants to light his pipe. That is the literal action. As a director it is important that you provide a literal physical action for each beat transition. If you do not consider what this literal action is then you run the risk of a static transition.

Russian theater director and actor Constantin Stanislavski noted that the most important element of his acting technique was playing a physical action. By that he meant not only the literal, but the essential. What is the essential action of what the character is doing in the scene? Once you know what the character is literally doing, the next step is choosing the essential action, or essence, of what the character is doing in the beat or scene. Take the man above searching for his tobacco. His essential action is to smoke one more pipe before he gives it up forever; or he could be stalling because after this pipe is finished, he will be leaving for prison. "I want to keep at bay my incarceration until the very last moment." This would be his essential action. It has to do with inner desire. It has to do with feelings and needs. It is what motivates him to slowly search the room for his smoking materials. These two things, literal and essential action, are going on here simultaneously. They take form during the beat transition. They define the physical action and the internal motivation for the action of the beat and sometimes the entire scene.

As a director I always try to communicate to an actor that they should be playing two things at any one time. If the actor is realizing both the physical action and the essential action she deepens the performance; it assures that subtext will be played; and it can heighten the tension in a scene because the two actions can be opposed to each other. You are providing the story tools to your cast for which they will be grateful.

Sometimes in a new beat there is not an essential action. You are in a room, about to drink a glass of lemonade, and a wild man with a machete comes through a door and tries to remove your head. A mad chase begins. Well, all you are doing is instinctively trying to save your life which is not much of an essential action from the standpoint of meaning. Another example, found in *A Streetcar Named Desire* (1947), Stanley, in a rage, calls for Stella, his wife. The literal action is that "Stanley wants to scream loud enough that his wife will hear and come home to him." His essential action is "I want to implore a loved one to give me another chance."

You indicate a new beat, implying a beat transition with //. Then, in the script, note down your literal and essential actions. Here is an example:

> // (*BILLYBOY comes out of the closet, with pieces of female clothing over shoulders, head, etc., startling MICAH.*)

> —Almost any time you have an entrance, a phone call, or an exit by a character that is in the action, you have a new beat. In this example you have MICAH'S literal action being to get BILLYBOY out of the apartment. His essential action is to establish dominance over BILLYBOY and to not let him know that he's scared—

MICAH: What the. . .? You been there all along?

BILLYBOY: Smelling the moth balls.

MICAH: Whadja hear?

BILLYBOY: I heard the pop of a champagne cork. I heard the rustle of underthings.

MICAH: It's just you and me now, buddy. Time's runnin' out. We got to get movin'.

BILLBOY: I heard hot breath over the prairie.

MICAH: Yeah, well, I always said you had an overactive imagination. That's one of her. . . thingys, on your head, take it off. The briefcase is on the sofa. . .

BILLYBOY: And lipstick is on the glass, see?

MICAH: O.K. There was a lady up here. Nobody you know and none of your business. It wasn't her. See. She gave me the key . . . to use, with this . . . with this other dame. How in hell's name did you get in?

BILLYBOY: *(flashing his fingers.)* Magic fingers. You taught me well. Grease job.

MICAH: You let me know what you're doing from now on, you understand? I don't like surprises. I'll get the case, and . . . we are on our way.

> *(MICAH starts for the door. BILLYBOY draws a pistol from an inner pocket, throws the glass so it smashes into the door.)* //

—NEW BEAT. Characterized by physical action and a change in who is driving the action as BILLYBOY takes over controlling the primary action beat. MICAH was not successful in establishing or ending his beat. BILLYBOY's literal action is to keep MICAH from leaving. His essential action is to make MICAH know that he (BILLYBOY) is in control now and that he's dangerous. —

BILLYBOY: Shut the door. Turn around, slowly. Sit down. You're not going anyplace.

Plot Points

Story structure is based on the logical and meaningful construction of beats, which lead to scenes, which then leads to sequences and Acts. The milestone events, reversals, changes, conflicts, and resolutions that shape your story are called plot points. They represent those intense places in your play where your central character's goal or objective is challenged and is confronted with obstacles that must be overcome or the story will not move forward. These obstacles challenge the character's personal, relational, and environmental encounters in a progressively more complicated manner and ultimately provide the elements which will test the central character's worth. Determining the events or decisions that escalate a story's problem should be a primary job in script analysis for the director.

The narratives in Scripture are based essentially on *plot points*. Stories in the Word are structured around the key moments in the character's life. Joseph dreams, is thrown down a well, has various slave and prison encounters, and ends up facing the repercussions of the inciting incident in the Act Three climax when he faces his brothers. All these key life changing moments are what drive the story telling narrative of Scripture's primary characters.

Inciting Incident and Act One Climax

The *inciting incident*, or *point of attack*, is the scene where the action that defines the problem first coalesces. It is the beginning of the point of no return for your protagonist, in which he is confronted with a problem and must take action. It foreshadows and makes the Act Three climax of your play inevitable. In other words, the problem that the point of attack poses must be answered or at least addressed in some manner by the climax. The objective that the main character has at the point of attack must be satisfied in some way by the Act Three climax. The point of attack for *Oedipus Rex* (c. 429 BC) is when he decides to take up the challenge of finding the killer of Laius. The climax of the play is the self-revelation that he is the killer. The point of attack often serves as a crisis moment that propels the play into the Act One climax, which launches the protagonist definitively on his journey.

Act Two Progressive Complication and Mid-Point Crisis

In the play the Second Act begins after the First Act climax. It continues through the *mid-point crisis* (intermission) and ends at the Act Two climax, fairly close to the end of the play. American author and screenwriting expert Syd Field places the mid-point crisis around page sixty, which basically means a real change in the story occurs, a new major obstacle, or a reversal perhaps, that ups the ante for the hero and raises the degree of difficulty for the solving of his problem.[3] Strategies are usually becoming more desperate, more varied, and hopefully the central character is moving ahead as he overcomes and confronts the antagonistic forces.

One of the more important moments in the story's action is the mid-point crisis which happens just before the play's intermission. Examples of the questions the audience asks themselves as they head out to the lobby are "how is he going to get the girl; how will he find out he's being set up; will he actually go to the FBI and become a double agent?"

If the play does not have an intermission, the dramatic event of the mid-point crisis should still exist because it serves as a major change or reversal plot point in the drama. Since the play is usually composed of fewer events than a film, having these crisis moments of revelation, set back, mystery, reversal, and new elements introduced are very important so that the drama is developing with progressive complications. A woman points a gun at a policeman chained in her basement whom she has essentially kidnapped. Blackout. Gun shot. Intermission. Did she shoot him? What is going to happen next? A good set up for a mid-point crisis will provide several compelling reasons for the audience to return after the intermission.

Often the mid-point crisis, in the spirit of most plot points, is characterized by physical action. The characters are doing something rather than just talking about how things are going. So meaningful physical action is something of a necessity. As the director you need to fully capitalize on the urgency of this moment.

Act Two Climax

> "And not only that, but we also boast in our sufferings, knowing that suffering produces endurance, and endurance produces character, and character produces hope, and hope does not disappoint us, because God's love has been poured into our hearts through the Holy Spirit that has been given to us."
>
> —Romans 5: 3–5 (NRSV)

The play's Act Two climactic scene usually happens after the progressive complication has brought the protagonist to the lowest point of his experience. Progressive complication defines the nature of evolving action. If it is not progressive, it is not moving forward but is usually repeating itself. It is not complicated unless the nature of the obstacles that the protagonist has to overcome are becoming more difficult both externally and internally. The Act Two Climax takes place about three-quarters of the way through the play. The protagonist has not been able to overcome her flaw yet, and it looks like she might not be able to. Plot development has resulted in putting her in a position where it looks like she will not accomplish her goal. But circumstances arise so that she can overcome the obstacles that seem to be beating her down. She is not saved by the cavalry, rather often by her own resources. The protagonist finds a strategy and renewed direction.

The Act Two climax serves as a crisis for your Act Three climax, which often results in the protagonist realizing her potential, facing her limitations, transcending them, and starting to find a new vision, and renewed purpose. It is often a point where the character seeks out higher, even supernatural solutions. She is now facing her greatest fear, though it is usually left to the Act Three climax for her to defeat this fear.

Christ's Act Two climax is Gethsemane and the crucifixion. It is the dark night of the soul: He is deserted, crying out to God, and under great physical torment. His Act Three climax is "He is risen indeed." The Act Two climax is about pain, emotion, and paradox. Of course, the paradox and irony of Christ's situation is that he is the King of the Jews and the Son of God being crucified.

In tragedy, the Act Two climax is the hero's realization that he has blown it. Looking at William Shakespeare for examples: Lear is driven mad with the loss of identity as a King and father; Othello is sure that Desdemona has betrayed him; Hamlet returns from his sea journey knowing that he is going to die. It is the moment when the hero questions his quest, when he doubts his resources, when he is physically compromised, when he doubts God. It is a moment when the central character can express anger, hurt, guilt, despair, and show more vulnerability than he has so far. It is also a moment when the audience can identify more personally with the character's plight than previously. Perhaps it is also the moment when the character's greatest fear looks like it just might triumph over him; and he begins to realize what flaw it is that will be his undoing. It is a time when he might confess deeper things to those around him. It is also a time when someone with insight, a guide in some way, will offer hard advice. Whatever the problem, he still must find the resources within and around himself to manage to begin the process of renewal and awakening that will provide the fortitude to overcome and proceed to the final climax in Act Three. So now armed with the truth about himself and his situation, he is equipped to pursue the quest to the battle at the end. How is this accomplished? The ending does not have to be victorious for it to be complete or ultimately satisfying. If he does fail, at least now he has developed the understanding to know that his sacrifice has ultimate meaning and worth. Lear is stripped of everything, but as he spends his last breath carrying Cordelia, his child, in his arms, he has found the ultimate meaning of who he is—no longer as a King but a father to his daughter. His friends watch as his spirit ascends to heaven.

Act Three Climax

The protagonist now ventures into the final battle, the final confrontation, the final testing of her will against the forces arrayed in opposition. She is equipped with new resolve, new strategies, with a clearer concept of what is wanted and what is needed. She has a renewed sense of dedication to "the good" and to benefitting the community. Of course, not every Act Three climax is composed of all these elements, but they represent a sample of the physical and moral elements that can be included. These are all triumphant expressions of a successful and meaningful quest by the central character. If she falls short or misses the mark, if the moment passes her by, or if she is unable to grab the prize, get the guy, overcome her flaw, or have a new perspective on the meaning of life, then all we can hope for is that she sees and understands her failure. Willy Loman in *Death of a Salesman* commits suicide at the recognition of his failure as a father, as a salesman, and as a husband. If we see our own failings in Willy and are motivated to change them, then the identification factor is successful. Hedda Gabler shoots herself in the head with the realization that all she has sought to possess and to rule over has been destroyed or has eluded her, and her only recourse is not to become a slave to a culture and to relationships that she abhors. Her escape is a cowardly one. Judas's betrayal sets off an unstoppable series of events that lead to the death of absolute good, and at the same time forecasts an ultimate victory that he is unable to celebrate.

In John Patrick Shanley's *Doubt* (2008), a parable that questions the power of accusation and of unqualified judgement, we consider the guilt or innocence of Father Flynn having a sexual relationship with a male student. In the end Sister Aloysius, who is unwavering in her condemnation of the priest, ultimately expresses doubts surrounding the allegations. It is the antagonist here who has the "ah-ha" realization that she might have been guilty of rigid moralizing, and that she should have honored, or at least explored more fully her feelings of doubt. In Aaron Sorkin's play version of *To Kill a Mockingbird* (2018), Tom Robinson is wrongly convicted by a white jury, but at the same time the lawyer Atticus brilliantly exposes the racial bigotry that rules in this small Alabama town in 1936. We do not get legal justice, but rather become aware of moral justice. The Act Three climax does not always guarantee success in the central character's final working out of his journey; but the insight gained by the audience should encourage a discovery of the truths and contradictions of how we live together. If the Act Three climax does not offer anything to ponder, to learn from, and to better our own lives as we look deeper into ourselves, our relationships, and our work, then its ultimate worth must be questioned. The Act Three climax is where the theme is worked out through action and deemed worthy or not.

Directing Plot Points

Your biggest challenge as a director is telling the story through the way you stage and conceive of plot point moments. An audience should be able to interpret and understand the play's meaning if they watched nothing but your plot point renditions. In directing these moments, it is important to keep some of the following considerations in mind.

- **Character Revelation**: Have you staged and focused the moments of realization and conviction by the main characters so that they are clearly understood by the audience? These scenes are often mini plays by themselves, with rising actions and culminating experiences. They have an intense build to them, with multiple reactions to what is transpiring. So slow down and take them apart beat by beat, spending more time on designing effective movement into climactic positions, and using line and eye focus as well as lighting isolation to highlight reactions and results.

- **Image Re-creation**: What is the imagery you established at the opening of your production? How has this been changed or amplified in the plot point moments, especially Act Three? *King Lear* (c. 1606) is on his throne to begin the play and in the end he holds his daughter Cordelia in a field as he dies. *Peer Gynt* (1876) celebrates his freedom by standing on a barrel and jumping off as he launches himself into his world travels. At his return home years later, the same barrel is in shambles as he attempts to get one last drink from its dregs in despair. Hedda brandishes her father's pistols with flagrant disdain at the top of the play, but mournfully holds one to her breast as she walks solemnly off to commit suicide at the end (*Hedda Gabler*, 1891). Sally Bowles, in my interpretation of the musical *Cabaret* (1966) began her journey as the vibrant, sexy, singer in the Kit Cat Club. Her final image, after aborting her baby and leaving Cliff, depicted her as a puppet manipulated by an elevated Emcee to indicate how she had sold out to the political climate as opposed to freely following her conscience. The point of attack is the beginning of a journey. The Act Three climax is the end for your protagonist. How can you establish actions and the use of props and set pieces that reflect this?

The Act Three climax is where the final conscious and unconscious objectives of the protagonist are tested and realized or fail. How have you created the right moment of self-awareness for your character to reveal this vulnerability? What are the focused actions that you have created that reveal this? Think about the images surrounding the cross. Christ's nakedness, Judas's self-realization and ultimate self-destruction, Peter's third denial of knowing Jesus—images and actions that tell the story with reverberating depth.

- **Beginnings and Endings:** An effective way of communicating the psychological journey of your characters in the play you are directing is to contrast what they were like physically at the top of your production to how they end up. *Macbeth* (1606) is a conquering warrior at the top, an angst-ridden fallen king at the end. Oedipus is a young vibrant strategically pro-active King at the beginning of his quest, and a fallen hero blinded through self-mutilation at the end. Blanche, in *A Streetcar Named Desire* is a self-confident Southern belle when she comes to live with Stanley and Stella; at the end she is half insane and incoherent.

- **Environmental Narrative:** The set can have an organic and storytelling life of its own. Sam Shepherd's *True West* (1980) creates a toaster strewn wasteland out of a cookie cutter Texas ranch house. When I directed Anton Chekhov's *Three Sisters* (1900) the set was used to show how the sisters were cast out of their house as their empty dreams of going to Moscow crumbled around them—from the living room, to the attic, the front porch, and yard, the final view of the façade is painted grey, with wood flaking off, boards missing, windows shuttered, and overall, a sense of desolation. In *Hamlet*, which I directed for the Three Rivers Shakespeare Festival, all the characters began the play in modern rehearsal dress. But as they gave themselves to the destiny of the play, which always ends with the overwhelming presence of death, they evolved into the costumed Renaissance characters they were playing. Hamlet himself was desperately attempting to find what play he was in, what role he was supposed to play. Was it a psychological play dealing with Oedipus complexes? Or was it more like a Spanish revenge tragedy? What about a political thriller of assassination and usurping of a throne and Queen? When Hamlet returns from the voyage to England, he knows his destiny is to be destroyed by Claudius. As he changes rehearsal costume into period garb and takes up his sword, the sense of his tragic entanglement and inevitability is assured.

- **Confronting the Antagonist**: The final Act Three climactic battle pits the protagonist of the story against his antagonist. The way that you stage this final conflict, the strategizing for position, for power, is what the audience has been waiting for. This is usually a supercharged moment. I like to think of it as if everyone were playing it on tiptoes. Every moment is electric. Every gesture is an expression of the wants and needs that have been thwarted and are now close to realization. Think in conflictual terms: a boxing ring, a gladiatorial moment, a duel, a bull fight, a race to the finish, a torture chamber, a moment when a person exceeds expectation, and a moment of emotional glory. Find the metaphors that best suit your understanding of the play's climactic offering. Run with them and push them further than you thought possible. Here are some plot points to show variations. In *The Glass Menagerie* (1944), the glass animals of Laura's collection are breakable. What else is? Encroaching Nazism in *Good* (1982) ends with Halder, a "good man," deciding who lives and dies at Auschwitz. How can the concentration camp take over the show from the opening images? Drugs and mistaken identities are at the core of *A Midsummer Night's Dream* (c. 1596), How far do you feel you can push this?

Is the theme or main idea of your story revealed through action during your Act Three climax? It should not be talked about or stated—it must be enacted. It is your job as the director to find the tapestry of gestures and physical relationships that will tell the story in a set of final images and actions that culminate in a picture of the theme of the play.

For Dr. Faustus, it is the realization that time is about to run out and that he faces the reality of eternal damnation. The final image of Peer Gynt peeling an onion and finding nothing at its core tells the story of his life's journey.

What elements of redemption can you reveal in this final climactic action? Perhaps your character now realizes that the working out of her story has been one of personal destiny fulfilled. Perhaps she has acquired an element of hope that goes beyond good luck or coincidence. Perhaps she now realizes she could not have done it by herself, that something more was needed, that she is not totally sufficient unto herself. Could she have experienced a mystery, something that cannot be explained but that makes her wonder about the deeper questions of why life is the way it is?

Character Arc and the Change Dynamic

Most drama features characters who change. As a director you need to be aware of the categories of change that influence what is a new direction, worldview, or personal insight. This means being able to identify these moments in the script and translate their importance into action and reaction. It is also worthwhile for the director to be familiar with the various dramatic genres, in terms of understanding how characters develop and change in everything from tragedy to romantic comedy to theater of the absurd, and more.

This process of change can be mapped out through the creation of a character arc for your protagonist. The idea of legitimate change is at the heart of *character arc*—otherwise there is not any change, just a shift in circumstances. The change we are looking for is in the character, because that is what gives him a new level of consciousness and sense of self which can justify the movement toward some sort of redemptive hope.

A common phrase that emerges from play and film writing texts is that "characters don't change." We are what we are and all our psychological tendencies are formed by the age of five. We do not change, we merely realize potentialities, fears, and traits that have always been buried within us. There is some truth here, but the Judeo-Christian worldview offers a very different concept of change in that "we become new creatures" who "are being changed into his likeness from one degree of glory to another; for this comes from the Lord who is the Spirit" (2 Cor. 3:18, NRSV). This transformational catalyst comes from without (Holy Spirit) and is directly tied to our faith stance and to the sanctified walk that we experience after salvation. How to depict and stage this reality is one of the great challenges of the Christian writer and director. Scripture tells us that Matthew dropped his tax collecting duties to follow Jesus; but we are not invited into the psychological and spiritual pressures that brought about this radical change in his life. But his actions tell us that something startling happened. Another rendition of change is shown through the depiction of Zacchaeus, also a tax collector, who in his overwhelming desire to see Jesus "runs" down the street and "climbs" a tree. He agrees to host Jesus for a meal, inviting all of his so-called sinner friends to come along, and the next morning he restores what he has stolen from people "fourfold" (Luke 19:1–10). Scripture does not provide us with a long monologue in which Zacchaeus tells us how he was "saved" by Jesus. Rather it demonstrates through a series of significant actions the state of his mind and his ultimate turnaround, the key to communicating this phenomenal change. In Charles Dickens's *A Christmas Carol* (1843), Scrooge does not stop to give us a treatise about how the visiting "spirits" changed his life. Rather he throws open the window to his cold apartment and buys a goose and Christmas presents for the Cratchits and for his family. In my play *Paper Wings* (1995), we watch Jamie's faith foundation grow and replace the emotional unrest which she displayed in Act One through a series of actions that speak to her new life in Christ. We know and ultimately believe a person not by their words but by their actions.

Are your characters pursuing an objective that will lead them toward a higher sense of virtue? In other words, are they pursuing a goal that challenges who they are at the beginning of the story, and which takes them through a journey that ends in the awareness that they are more valuable, and that life in general is worth more, than what they started with?

Sometimes this change results in negative values being brought to the surface rather than positive ones. Jonah, the reluctant prophet, is changed at the end of his Nineveh experience in being even more desultory in his personal relationship with God (Jonah 4:1–2). His inability to change and rejoice with the Ninevites is his curse. Michael Corleone in Francis Ford Coppola's *The Godfather: Part III* (1972) ends up having lost his personal sense of conscience. Each of these characters change, but rather than being for the better, the changes here portray characters who end up more destitute and lost in their disassociation from themselves and their surroundings. *Hedda Gabler* imagines herself as the head of a male worship cult and ends up committing suicide as she becomes trapped in her own misguided indulgences.

Character Arc and Emotional Change

Learning how to feel is a key element that indicates a process toward change. C. S. Lewis's love story in *Shadowlands* (1993) moves from retribution and anger to forgiveness and even shades of hope. Staunch materialist Mother Courage, in the play *Mother Courage and Her Children* (1939) by Bertolt Brecht, moves audiences to tears with her silent scream over the loss of her children. Moving from hope to despair is the path that Samuel Beckett lays out for his lost clowns in *Waiting for Godot* (1952).

Character Arc and Cultural Change

The poet who becomes a businessman in Mohsin Hamid's novel *The*

Reluctant Fundamentalist (2007), the erudite professor who falls in love with the male nurse as she is dying of cancer in *Wit* (1999), the working-class English student who ends up transcending her instructor in *Educating Rita* (1981), and the steelworker who ends up building a cathedral in my play *Miracle Mile* (2008) are all examples of characters triumphing in areas that are challenging and not anticipated. As a director you are responsible for knowing the cultural context from which your play has been created. This more likely than not requires research into the historical, familial, philosophical, and environmental cultures that frame the drama you are bringing to life.

When directing Shakespeare's *The Merchant of Venice* (1605), I immersed myself in a study of the Jewish ghettos in Italy of that period and staged it during the carnival. And yet, the play could and has been set in Germany in pre-World War II times, which would then require an understanding of the class systems and European Jewish culture of that period.

Character Arc and Ethical Change

If the character arc is doing what it is supposed to do, the primary characters will often discover a deeper reason for why they are pursuing their goals. This involves moral or ethical change. Natural law is imprinted by God in our hearts, directing both us and the dramatic characters toward a hoped-for natural good. The worlds of film and theater more often than not forbid looking at incest, murder, or adultery as positive forces. Where is your character as an ethical being at the beginning and where are they at the end of the play? For example, Caesar, the hero ape in *War for the Planet of the Apes* (2017), begins his journey seeking revenge but ends up showing mercy on his antagonist and becoming the savior for his community. The character's discovery often involves a revelation about himself, about his potential that has lain dormant, and the resultant "ah hah" moment caps the character arc. Such is the moment when the troublemaker McMurphy in the film *One Flew Over the Cuckoo's Nest* (2010) sacrifices himself for a select number of inmates at a repressive mental asylum.

Character Arc and Family Change

Changes in family dynamics also play an important role in the character's story arc. In dramatic works, some families are destroyed while others flourish. A family traditionally shares goals, values, and long-term commitments. It represents one of the basic building blocks of dramatic writing. And family moves easily into representative forms: the family as a sports team; the extended family that can exist in trailer parks; surrogate families that come about when diverse characters are placed in high conflict situations. The pursuit of completing missing elements in the family structure is a common subconscious desire within a protagonist or antagonist. An example is Edward Albee's *Who's Afraid of Virginia Woolf?* (1962) in which a two-person family tears itself apart and then, with what love remains, puts itself back together in a different way. In Eugene O'Neill's *Long Day's Journey into Night* (1941), the family is on the verge of collapse, and we watch with trepidation as we discover the secrets and misunderstandings that propel it to its final point of separation. In Scripture, Joseph faces his brothers in Egypt and forgives them in a moving scene of confrontation and forgiveness. This family then becomes a nation.

Character Arc and Physical Change

Finally, in terms of character arc, look for changes in the physicality of your characters. How does their dress, their new relationships, their acquired changes in perspective manifest both in the character's own physical presence as well as their physical environment? David transforms from shepherd to King. Prince Hal in Shakespeare's *Henry IV, Part 1* (1597) transforms from disreputable Prince to proper Prince. Lear, the King, is stripped of all royal trappings by the end of the play and is left only the role of repentant father. Stanley, the prodigal musician, ends up leaving his escapist pajamas and being brutally dressed in formal clothes while in a catatonic freeze at the end of Harold Pinter's *The Birthday Party* (1957).

Character Arc and Character Flaw

What is the character up against, not only externally but internally in terms of a *character flaw*? What is that flaw? What is keeping the character from getting what he wants? How has he dealt with this flaw by the end of the piece? This uniquely human factor in your story can be at the heart of your protagonist's journey. Her ability to overcome her flaw or to make positive use of it is an important dramatic element. Hedda's flaw in *Hedda Gabler* is that she wants to control the lives of everyone around her. Her flaw gets the best of her; and she cannot face a life that makes her a victim rather than a perpetrator. In Sophocles's *Oedipus Rex*, Oedipus's flaw is pride, for which he is humbled, but in the process finds his true humanity. Sally's flaw in *Cabaret* is that she cannot give up the adoration she receives at the Kit Kat Club. In the end she sacrifices her child, loses her love, and condemns herself to a life performing for a corrupt German society. Often the measure of the character is in how he succeeds or not in overcoming his flaw in the Act Three climax. God's revelation of character flaws in scriptural characters is unique in contrast to other religious books. Abraham, Joseph, David, Gideon, Jonah, Jezebel and Ahab, Michel, Moses, Rahab, Peter, Thomas, Paul, and others all exhibit character traits that could be seen as character flaws that motivate action and that are addressed in God's unfolding story in Scripture.

Character Arc and Change in Consciousness

As a species we are blessed with various attributes that reflect our being made in God's image, one of these being a change in consciousness. These are qualities that I believe are at the heart of effective change within individual or societal units and are worthy to pursue in awakening God consciousness in your treatment of characters and in your audiences. Some of these could include:

- Awakening **self-consciousness** through having your characters pursue questions of identity: Who am I? Why am I here? What do I want? How can I change my circumstances for the greater good? These questions are at the heart of ultimate purpose and meaning in life.

- Is there an **enhanced responsiveness** to beauty and the call of moral responsibility for one's actions?

- Is there an **envisioning of a future** and developing the potential acts to change it? Is there the ability to love each other, even to the point of self-sacrifice?

- Is there a **sense of cause and effect**, of destiny beyond oneself, which one pursues with all his or her will? To seek the mysteries of existence that go beyond our present temporal and spatial boundaries is built into the fabric of human consciousness.

As is evident, these are all Christ-like attributes. He is the answer to the searching questions of our lives. He is perfection. He is the future. He is the standard bearer for true love of others; and he provides us with a sense that we belong to his Kingdom and will participate in it for all of eternity.

The world of character creation is peopled with an endless variety of types, of contrasting personalities, of noble and less noble goals, of the revelation of human truths, and of the search for representational and symbolic truth. All this is exhibited through characters who are capable of love, sacrifice, while equally capable of self-centered destructiveness. The Christian virtues, to be proved meaningful, need to be challenged by our baser instincts; otherwise finding and holding them up as meaningful standards of relationships and ultimate goals becomes trite. This dichotomy needs a director at the helm who understands the ethical heart of the play and the moral directives of Scripture. Not only must the values be understood as they change and challenge the characters, but the competent director has to sense when these moments of acquired consciousness happen and how to amplify and focus them through action, movement, props, and reactions.

Discussion Questions and Exercises

1. **Identifying and Labeling Beats in Action**. Select a scene from a play of your choice that has two or more characters. This could also be a play that you are writing or planning to direct. Identify the following:

   - Mark the beats by using // for each beat transition.
   - Identify the beats as action or mood.
   - Identify who is *driving* the beat. If the main *driver* of a beat loses that domination, you usually have a new beat as another character takes over to drive the beat.

2. **Literal and Essential Actions**. Every beat transition has both a Literal and Essential Action happening in it and both serve to guide the development in the scene you are working on. Take the scene above in which you identified the beats and within the beat transition write down in the margin the Literal and Essential Actions. So, what you are recording is the blocking or movement *and* the personal motivation for the action.

3. **Plot Points**. In a play of your choice identify the major plot points, i.e., Inciting Incident, Act One Climax, Mid- Point Crisis, Act Two Climax, Act Three Climax. Justify your selection of each plot point by providing the reasons why you selected the dramatic moments that you did.

4. **Theme**. In your Act Three climax your theme should be realized through actions, discoveries, secrets revealed, and heightened consciousness by the protagonist. It can be considered to be meaning-in-action. In three plays analyze how the theme is realized in your Act Three climax as image and action—not as stated but as experienced.

5. **Act Three**. Climax and Denouement. Usually, the various plot points involve a decision that is made that can change the direction of the play's story. A character is changing his mind, discovering something new, overwhelmed at self or other revelation. What happens to the inner rhythm, focus, intention, energy, and physicality involved in the Act Three climax? Using the three plays used above, how can you realize new consciousness through props, movement, breath, making it visual and not just an internalized understanding? Describe in writing and then coach an actor in realizing this highly personal moment.

6. **Character Arc and Cultural Awareness**. Using a play of your choice, research into the historical, familial, philosophical, and environmental cultures that frame the drama you are bringing to life. An example might be Tennessee Williams's *A Streetcar Named Desire*. It is set in New Orleans in the summer, in a working-class neighborhood. The heat is oppressive. Tenement socializing is prevalent. Male ego and male dominance rule. What is the social environment that Blanche comes out of? What do the clothes in the 1940s say about the people and the environment? How noisy is the place? How private? How does this front porch environment work? How does this crowded place become a cauldron for sensory exploration? Have you listened to the jazz coming out of these environs? Will the blues work in this story? How do you bring these things to life in your production?

7. **Character Arc as a Paradigm for Change**. Selecting either the protagonist or antagonist in a play of your choice apply the character arc determinates as outlined in the book as a methodology for analysis. This would include applying the following change categories to your character's arc or journey:

- Emotional Change
- Cultural Change

- Moral or Ethical Change
- Family Change
- Physical Change
- Self-Consciousness Change

Chapter 6

Preparatory Work After Script Analysis

YOU HAVE BROKEN THE SCRIPT DOWN into motivational beats. You have analyzed image progression. You have identified the plot points and how they work. You have put your characters through the rigors of character arc analysis. You have researched the cultural and environmental worlds of your play's context or form. Now it is time to begin the preparatory work that will translate these plot and character progressions into a stage-worthy vehicle.

For the director, this involves creating a workable ground plan of appraising the positive and negative aspects of the stage space and communicating the scenic design concept and character details to the set, lighting, and costume designers. It also involves putting the above elements and more into the bible of your production: the prompt book.

The Idea of Space

An empty stage is essentially a neutral spatial area that is crying out for expression, to be filled with emotion, movement, and meaning. Do you envision how this space will be utilized to communicate a statement in terms of your production concept?

It helps the director to become acquainted with the artistic history and practices involved in all great art movements as well as contemporary culture. Study the great Renaissance painters and note how they focus space through background and foreground elements of action. Note how their frame of action is not contained wholly in itself but spills imaginatively beyond the frame of the picture. How is the action of the painting emphasized through color, through mass, contrast, texture, focus light and shadow? Note the figures and movement within these great paintings. If they came to life, would the subjects have directed movement toward and away from each other? In other words, the composition or stage picture is never totally stagnant, but is always pushing to find the next picture.

One of the techniques used to capture kinetic energy in stage compositions is the creation of an asymmetrical tension, or a picture that is out of balance. Conflict is the essential ingredient that makes a playscript work; so is it with your design concept. If you start off with total symmetry, the challenge then is to find ways of destroying this as the play progresses. If you cannot do this with the material construction elements, then be sure to do it with props, movable set pieces, and blocking and compositional tension. One element to think about is internal framing devices that can be flown in and out as well as the use of doors, windows, and lighting emphasis. Ask yourself how the space reflects the play's action by either working with it or against it. How does it reflect or contradict and work against the protagonist's objective? An example from the musical *Hadestown* (2016) is the use of a series of turntables that rise and fall beneath the stage level, emphasizing the hero's journey to hell and back as a cyclical nightmare.

In his book *A Grammar of Motives*, American literary theorist and author Kenneth Burke provides a heady examination of framing dynamics in his discussion about scene/act ratio. He demonstrates how dramatic tension and meaning in Shakespeare comes from the various scenes juxtaposing different locations in terms of size, weight, height, and movement.[1] Russian filmmaker, Sergei Eisenstein, does the same for the film genre in his book, *Film Form and Film Sense.*[2] Closely examine the psychological and physical journey of your protagonist and find equivalencies that reflect this in the scenic progression. The word "progression" is used to emphasize that a set can evolve along with emotional and thematic elements of the action.

Knowing the exigencies of the stage space that you will be mounting your production on is a key consideration in the preparatory work that the director must accomplish. Visit the theater if you are not familiar with it. Spend a good deal of time walking through the on-stage and off-stage working spaces. Check the auditorium seating for sightlines. Look at the tech booths for visibility and soundproofing. How many follow spotlights can be mounted and used effectively? What is the composition of the stage floor? How many permanent entrances and exits are there onto the stage proper (stage right, stage left, up stage) and from the auditorium? Check the auditorium for echo factors; sound quality is as important as visibility. Is the fly space, or rigging system, adequate and workable? How many lines are there? Is there an orchestra pit? Are there workable trap doors? What about the wings and supportive curtain drops? And most importantly, talk with producers, prior directors, designers, actors, and stage managers to determine what the advantages and pit falls of the space might be and how they tried to overcome apparent deficiencies in previous productions.

Proscenium Stage

The most used stage space arrangement is the *proscenium stage*. The proscenium arch is a picture frame stage featuring a large opening, with the audience all facing the stage in the same direction. It is the least dimensional of all the stage spaces and requires more technical and design elements to mask the offstage areas.

Hopefully it will feature an *apron*, which is a small acting area constructed to bring the playing elements out toward the audience in front of the proscenium arch. Sight lines should be determined by sitting in the furthest front row seats (left and right) in the auditorium. Draw intersecting lines from there to the furthest back wall of the stage space and you will understand the space context that you must work in. This will establish the parameters of where your set can be located. The area within the lines is your main design and acting area.

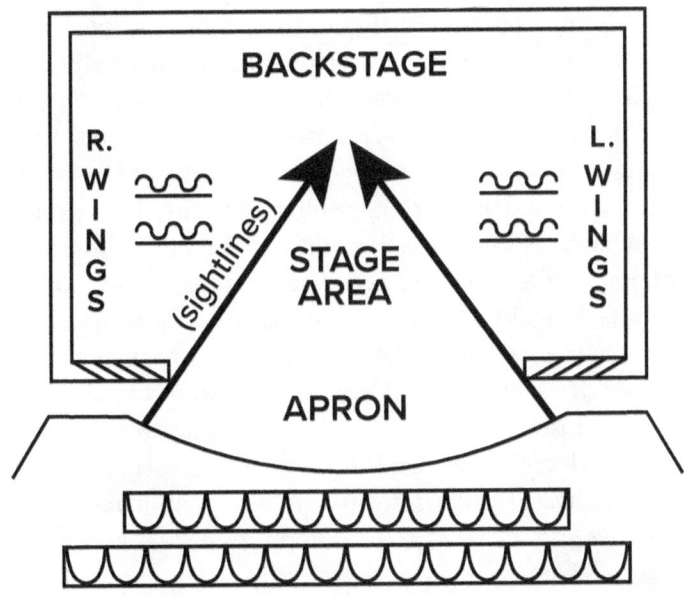

Figure 1. Proscenium stage. Original drawing by Gillette Elvgren. Used with permission.

Are the wing spaces adequately masked? How much of the upstage left and right areas on stage can be clearly seen (remember *upstage* signifies the area at the back of the stage, farthest away from the audience)? Does the proscenium vertical span cut off the sight lines from the upper tiers of the balcony? Does the apron extend too far into the auditorium so that the balcony audiences cannot see the action staged there? Is there enough wing space (the backstage areas on the left and right of the stage, unseen to the audience) to store props and set pieces used in scene transitions?

The proscenium stage is best suited to create the illusory effects of realism in that it can hide most of the theatrical mechanisms. A curtain can descend to hide the act and scene changes, though hopefully it does not. Actors can appear and disappear with more facility. Platforms, second-story rooms and areas also involve the need for space dedicated to escape steps and platforming. From the standpoint of blocking, know that you will be working with actors to remind them to turn downstage when moving and to open up when making exits to upstage areas. This is an artificial solution to sight line problems, but if done well will hardly be noticed.

The strongest crosses are diagonal from upstage right (UR) to downstage left (DL), but any cross that goes toward the audience will be the strongest in terms of focusing a meaningful action in the script.

It is also essential to motivate the downstage areas. Directors too often make the mistake of creating a ground plan that puts most of the action upstage, which reduces strong crosses downstage by bringing the action closer to the audience. It is too commonplace to have a proscenium stage with an apron, but not have any set pieces on the apron to motivate the most important area of the stage. And be sure to create enough of an obstacle course to make all crosses effective. An actor communicates her objectives by the way she drags her hand along the back of a sofa or goes to get another drink at the bar down left. Any form of creating conflict in space helps to reveal character. Breaking up long crosses with set and personnel obstacles is recommended. If an apron is used, then your problem is again motivating moves down onto it. Not utilizing the apron for climactic scenes and such will give the impression of looking at a production through a telescope.

One thing to be aware of in a proscenium theater is the audible limitations. Actor training has largely given up on teaching voice production, so mics are used far too often especially on the proscenium stage. Regrettably, even smaller theater arrangements make flagrant use of microphones. When directing on the proscenium, I always go to the back of the auditorium and make notes about audibility.

Crowd scenes are most effective on the proscenium stage as opposed to the thrust and arena stage spaces. Crowds go offstage to create the illusion of size, and the vertical use of platforming adds dynamic compositional emphasis to telling the story. It requires one to be familiar with the observations on how to direct crowd scenes in *Directors on Directing* by Cole and Chinoy. Such techniques as breaking the crowd up into smaller motivational and culturally identifiable groups, assigning each group a separate agenda, the use of pertinent props, and verbal coaching in terms of diverse group reactions are all discussed in the chapter by the Duke of Saxe-Meiningen.[3]

Arena Stage

The *arena stage*, or *theater-in-the-round*, is another type of theatrical venue that has a variety of positive factors working for it as a counter to the proscenium stage. Since it is surrounded by the audience, elaborate scenery is seldom a consideration and risers or platforms can be used, but only minimally. The entrances are through the audience or a *vomitorium* (like a football stadium), and the number of front row seats are increased considerably over the proscenium. It is a more intimate environment. Since the audience is in such close proximity, the detailed work on set pieces, costumes, and props needs to be finely crafted. One of the primary design elements is the floor design.

Movement does not need to be toward the audience, so it has an authenticity to real life in terms of physical relationships and patterns of movement. Instead of directing an actor to move upstage right, he would be told to cross to two o'clock. Some directors use compass delineations to communicate direction: "move southwest toward the door." The imaginative use of sound and lights becomes extremely important as a scenic component because of the restrictions on set pieces. Furniture must be low in silhouette so as not to block the sight lines of first row audience participants. The stage itself is often elevated by up to 18 inches or more and the rake of the orchestra seats is steeper than in more traditional theater architecture.

Flying actors is difficult, though they can be raised or lowered from the catwalk above.

Lighting must shine three-dimensionally on each stage element, including actors, so the number of lights is often increased and brought closer to the working stage area than in larger proscenium theaters.

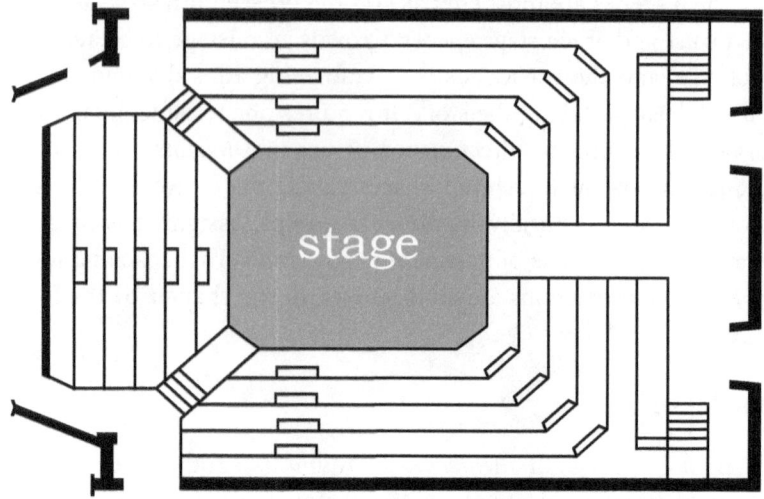

Figure 2. Theater in the Round, Victoria Theater, Stoke-on-Trent. Courtesy of Becky Loton. Used with permission.

The arena stage is good for multi-scene plays that move rapidly. When I spent almost a year at the arena stage in Stoke-on-Trent in the Midlands in England, I talked with several of their playwrights who liked writing for the arena stage because it is like the stage is a depiction of their mind, where anything can happen in an effortless fashion. Characters can be flying in an airplane and the next moment be on a mountain top, with nothing more than lighting and a sound effects change. The script becomes paramount rather than spectacle with a lot of burdensome sets moving about.

An arena arrangement is also a wonderful space to stage children's theater in which the audience is even asked selectively to come up on the stage. Easy access and the intimacy of the stage is less imposing to the younger audience.

The arena stage is more of an actors' theater. It is usually less expensive to design for and the designs can be toured in a more accessible way. Some of the drawbacks for the arena type of staging are as follows:

- Lighting the action three-dimensionally without throwing light on the first few rows surrounding the stage is a challenge.

- Scene transitions and moving props, set pieces, and furniture on and off between scenes can be laborious and time consuming. The director needs to make these moves *a vista,* or in view of the audience, so they need to be entertaining and hopefully related to the action of the show. So in Chekhov, perhaps, scene changers would resemble peasants or servants who are made to work in a disgruntled fashion to change their master's environments. In other words, these changes need to be organic to the story. The biggest mistake is to fade to black and let the audience guess what is going on with the inevitable clinks and thump sounds which are made by stagehands who are dressed in black and trying unsuccessfully not to be seen. No scene change should take more than twelve seconds. And if it does, then it should be incorporated into the visual and dramatic style of the production itself.

- Actors find that they must learn to act with their backs to communicate to at least a third of the audience either what they are saying or reacting to because their faces cannot be seen. Reactions should be magnified vocally and physically to be seen and heard, or at least guessed at by the audience. And the talent must learn to not stay still for long periods of time. Opening up the actors' silhouettes is an on-going process. The director also needs to look at the scenes he is working on from several different viewpoints, walking around the seating area to critique the visibility of moments. Actors have commented that when doing a more intimate or romantic scene that being so close to the audience has meant that they try to forget the audience and play into their partner. This can compromise the need to share any moment as much as possible through movement and emphasis with the entire audience. An actor sitting in a chair will need to alter his positioning in it to obtain different looks.

- Staging musicals and farces also present unique challenges. Choreography is most often designed for a single audience focus as well as are solo musical numbers. How to play the musical to four sides is no easy task. Farces often demand moments where characters are hiding behind curtains or doors, overhearing something said on stage. So know that hidden and surprise entrances are difficult to pull off. Along those lines, trying to project visuals on screens is difficult, and is often best accomplished by hanging screens behind and elevated above each of the audience seating areas. Finally, I suggest not putting a table, round or otherwise, in the exact center of the arena stage, because the tendency then will be to create movement patterns that seem to move endlessly around it. There is also a tendency to place all the furniture around the edge of the stage. Avoid doing this. It is so artificial. You have a natural room environment, so make it organic.

Thrust Stage

There are some variants to these spaces and the *thrust stage* remains an interesting compromise between the two already discussed. It has a backstage design component like the proscenium, with the intimacy of theater-in-the-round.

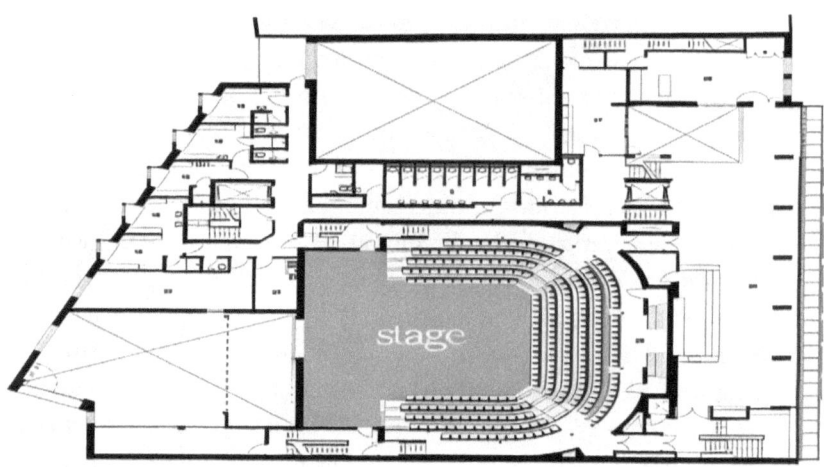

Figure 3. Everyman Theater, Liverpool, England. Architect: Haworth Tompkins. Used with permission of Gemma Murrell.

Usually there are four guaranteed entrances to the stage in the thrust arrangement, two through the vomitorium and at least two from the up-stage area that can be masked. Its advantages are all of those of the arena staging, with the added ingredient of having a more fixed design compo-nent upstage with the ability to fly a limited number of drops and where platforms can be built that flow into the thrust stage environment below what could be called the proscenium.

Motivating the downstage area is the challenge. Shakespeare did it for his Globe theater productions by writing lines long enough to carry the ac-tor down on entrances and back again on exits. The stage should be higher than the front row of seats to enable good sight lines, but not high enough to make the audience crane their necks looking up at the action.

The Ground Plan

When communicating with my stage designer, I always bring several copies of an overview of the stage space, and I often have one or more ground plan conceptions that I have already worked out. I firmly believe that the director holds the trump card in determining the nature of the ground plan. You have usually spent a lot of time developing your concept and imagining the movement patterns, props, and set pieces. To say to a designer, "*The Cherry Orchard* is coming up, let's see what you can come up with" is handing the designer a *carte blanche*, or blank check, from the standpoint of artistic ownership of the production. You are the expert in ground plans. You are the one who has to make them work in the designated space. I even show the designer my rudimentary drawings of what I think the set should look like in perspective. And I show them doodles I have made in the prompt book of props, set pieces, or a visual concept of the characters. Most designers appreciate this rough visual input. It excites their imagination and gets the process going. But know that things will change, so be open to it. What changes?

Producers say it is too expensive. Designers say there is not enough wing space or that they do not have the labor force to pull off the decorative elements and the construction needs. Compromise is the apt word for this on-going process of give and take with the technical and design personnel. What do you need to be aware of when creating a workable ground plan? The following provides the Where, When, Who, What, and Why elements, or the *given circumstances* that need to be considered in putting together this important visual document. A series of questions about other elements are provided to establish the context of your play's world. These reminders will help you in being able to dictate the parameters of your production concept. Getting halfway through a rehearsal process and realizing that the ground plan or production concept does not work is what needs to be avoided at all costs.

Where?

Where is your geographical location? Have you researched the different environmental differences between, let's say, Norway, Russia, or South Africa? What is the neighborhood like? What is next door or down the road? Is the feel of the place roomy, cramped, sentimental, barren, messy, smelly. . . what? Find the adjectives. What exterior light sources are there? Streetlights, neon signs, the moon, the sun, car lights? Is the neighborhood threatening, open, friendly, isolated, decaying, new, old? If you have an interior set like the cheap and tacky Bed and Breakfast seaside environment for Harold Pinter's *The Birthday Party* (1959) and you place it in a stylish Myrtle Beach condo, what have you sacrificed? If Nora lives in a traditional low ceilinged Norwegian middle-class house, and you put her in an expansive vaulted gothic Victorian house, what impact does that have in Henrik Ibsen's *A Doll's House* (1879)?

When?

What is the date, season, or time of the day for each scene and what have you done to establish this? Ask yourself what effect these given circumstances have on the characters throughout the drama. How does your set and ground plan(s) reflect and serve these potential environmental changes? If you are doing a period play, then have you researched the dress, the cultural life, the entertainment forms, and characteristics to make the setting happen with authenticity? If you have modernized the time period, have you found corresponding set, prop, and costume usages that will reflect the original intention of the playwright's story?

Who and What?

Where, and to what extent, were your characters educated? What class do they consider themselves to be? What habits or hobbies do they have? What foods do they like? What are they in revolt against culturally, personally, or professionally? How does your environment help, reflect, or hinder communicating these aspects? What are the characters' relationships to the space they find themselves in? Are they intruders? Do they want to be there? How at ease are they? Have they been here before? Perhaps one character wants to dominate another. They might do this by taking over the favorite chair, desk, side bar of the other character. Ask yourself how they might want to use the space. Find a metaphor: are they holding court, having a contest comparable to a sporting event, involved in a seduction, or planning to undercut and belittle? How can your environment also help or play against these impulses?

Why?

Ask yourself why the writer chose to put these characters together in this environment at this time. What is the nature of the conflict being played out and why is it being realized in this place? For example, you are directing a farce which has a wild chase in a china shop; think of the comic possibilities and the tension that can ensue. The environment might present natural obstacles to the action that is being played out. Well-kept Felix comes to live in a messy apartment with Oscar the slob in *The Odd Couple* (1965). The place is designed with the conflict that will occur in mind. Ask yourself what normally goes on in this environment, a nursing home, a drawing room, classroom, or cave? What counter activities has the playwright created that play against the normal expectations of what occurs in an upper-class drawing room? Hedda Gabler points a gun in a drawing room at Judge Brack. Aristophanes' hell, in *The Frogs* (405 BC), has Xanthias and Dionysus demonstrate a wide range of hilarious farcical routines. In Henry Living's *Eh?* (1966), the boiler in the basement makes a cacophony of sounds and light effects that raise it to the level of having personified qualities. It becomes like a second character onstage. How does the environment evolve? How does it change? Have you allowed for all these scene transitions?

Some Practical Considerations

The ground plan must serve you, the script, and your interpretation of it. It also must serve the space it is conceived in and make organic sense. Some questions you might consider are provided. How many acting areas does your ground plan have? It is recommended that you have no less than five. An empty stage has as many as you want to bring to it. A character with an umbrella miming the rain is creating a space. What defines an acting area? A space where definitive action usually takes place. It can be undesignated by set pieces such as the downstage center area where climactic moments often arise. It is usually defined by exit and entrance areas or around objects like a fireplace, a piano, a sofa, a chair, and the like. These areas should motivate reasons to move from one to another. Mom always sits on the sofa with a footstool and a side table for her sewing. It is a kind of work area. George has his library nook where he retreats to his books when things get too volatile. Martha loves her bar, makes all the drinks and does it with style, always having one in hand as she moves out into the scene.

Think in terms of levels. They help constitute meaningful and visually exciting compositions and offer an alternative to the flat movement patterns of a stage. Can you foresee a sunken living room? Stairs, landings, balconies, trees to climb, porches, and so forth add to the energy of your staging.

Where do your entrances and exits go to and come from? How can you establish this? These provide natural framing devices to highlight stage pictures and to focus on what is oftentimes a new beat transition when characters use them. Your ground plan should feature a visual representation of your set that indicates where these entrance and exit areas are and how they logically function. On it you also indicate the placing, height, and escape mechanisms from your platforming and stairs. What considerations do you make in terms of your furniture placement? How does it reflect the movement patterns and potential of the characters who move through it? Grandma's living room is filled with stacks of magazines and old newspapers and everything else that she just cannot throw out. How does this function as a wonderful, organic repository for props to be used as her story is told in her space? Is your furniture hugging the walls or is it placed so that as acting areas actors can move in, on, and around these pieces? Have you allowed for diagonal motivated crosses from up to down stage areas? At the same time have you created a believable obstacle course of objects and furniture that assist your actor to tell his story during movement sequences? Have you found the imbalance or asymmetrical tension in your ground plan? The decorative nature of realizing your ground plan is the function of the designers. The movement and storytelling potential of your ground plan is created by you.

Here are some points about the sample ground plan below. With a ruler, some graph paper, and a little practice you can complete something quite similar.

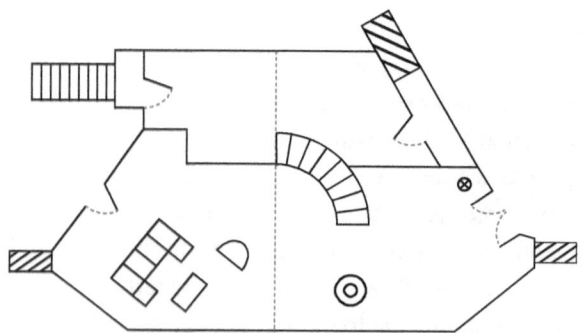

Figure 4. Ground plan sketch by Gillette Elvgren.
Used with permission.

This ground plan has a short apron downstage of the proscenium arches (indicated by ////) and the sofa helps to motivate that area. There are four entrance/exits altogether which is more than sufficient. Escape steps are also drawn in. Acting areas would be the entrances, the sofa, the table, and perhaps the poof/stool. Notice how doors open down to upstage and escape steps are indicated. Finally, there is a stairway and a four-foot-high platform to provide sculpting and height. Your designer will provide you with scale drawings, but this is the kind of input to the designers that they will appreciate.

The Prompt Book: Two Versions— Director's and Stage Manager's

The *prompt book* is the most important comprehensive document that the director creates. It is literally his Bible to the production concept and execution, incorporating the script, blocking, ground plans, beat transitions, and drawings, doodles, or whatever works for your particular artistic style. I include copies of research notes that I find pertinent and pictures that stimulate my imagination. If you lose this document halfway through the directing process, you will most likely feel that it is time to take the next train out of town. You will find that as the show progresses, you will literally be carrying this book around with you everywhere, spilling food and coffee on it, and watching it get impossibly large and exhaustive.

It should be noted that there are usually two prompt books: the one referred to above and the stage manager's prompt book. In the latter, the stage manager records all blocking, and places all cues for lights, sound, and notes about what will be broadcast over backstage audio to notify actors of entrances. She uses this to call all the cues in the show to the tech crew. The director's prompt book is personal and includes all the essential information mentioned above in terms of blocking, personal notes, beats, research, and working ground plan. A workable approach to putting this director's prompt book together should incorporate the following elements.

The first thing is to copy the script so that there is a blank page on the back of every page entry. This is done so as you turn the page of the prompt book, you are faced on the left with an empty page and on the right the next page of the script itself. The first pages of the book before your script is introduced could include your research notes that you want to refer to during the directing process; relevant photos; a designer's rendering of your ground plan (1/4" = 1'); frontal drawings in perspective of the designer's rendering; a prop list; central image concept; and a directory of designer, tech, and acting personnel phone numbers and email addresses. Also, weekly rehearsal schedules should be included. It is also recommended to note Scripture verses that you find most applicable to the process that you are going through such as:

"Whatever you do, work heartily, as for the Lord and not for men."—Col. 3:23 (ESV)

"Do you see a man skillful in his work? He will stand before kings; he will not stand before obscure men."—Prov. 22:29 (ESV)

"Do not be conformed to this world, but be transformed by the renewal of your mind, that by testing you may discern what is the will of God, what is good and acceptable and perfect."— Rom. 12:2 (ESV)

"For nothing will be impossible with God."—Luke 1:37 (ESV)

"But now, O Lord, you are our Father; we are the clay, and you are our potter; we are all the work of your hand."—Isa. 64:8 (ESV)

"To the choirmaster. A Psalm of David. O Lord, you have searched me and known me! You know when I sit down and when I rise up; you discern my thoughts from afar. You search out my path and my lying down and are acquainted with all my ways. Even before a word is on my tongue, behold, O Lord, you know it altogether. You hem me in, behind and before, and lay your hand upon me. . ."—Ps. 139:1–24 (ESV)

"According to the grace of God given to me, like a skilled master builder I laid a foundation, and someone else is building upon it. Let each one take care how he builds upon it."—1 Cor. 3:10 (ESV)

The script page is located on the right-hand page, copied to an appropriate size so you have room in the margins to write notes. On it you indicate a // marking for each beat. Each beat transition is identified with a beat objective for the dominant character. A list of appropriate objective-oriented words to consider can be found in William Ball's directing text *A Sense of Direction* (1984) or in Lajos Egri's *The Art of Dramatic Writing* (1946).[4] This is important because your blocking work with the actors will proceed from beat to beat. You will also indicate a blocking notation in the script. If, for example, you want Dan to rise and cross to piano, you put a number in the script which references your blocking sequence in the scene.

So, let's say the Dan cross is a (1). Each movement should have a literal and essential action notation on it to record the reason for the movement.

On the left page, you have a miniaturized ground plan rendering of the scene on which you record using a number and arrow the nature of your blocking notation.

The right page margins should include pertinent notes, questions, props, and eventually all of your lighting and sound cues and a script of the play. In addition, your character objectives are written in the script wherever there is a beat transition. In summary, on the right is your script with beat information and numbered notations where you are blocking characters, personal notes, and technical cues. On the left is a ground plan on which you note your blocking movements according to the referenced numbers.

LEFT PAGE: Miniature ground plan, hand drawn.

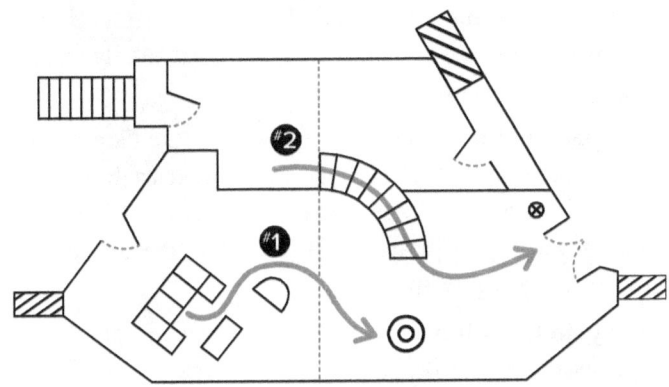

Figure 5. Groundplan sketch used in blocking a script by Gil Elvgren. Used with permission.

RIGHT PAGE of the Playscript:

> *(Doorbell rings. DAISY hears RALPH on landing and goes to her purse and cigarettes. Then sits on poof.) #1*

RALPH: Are you going to answer the doorbell?

DAISY: It's for you. It's always for you.

RALPH: Are you going to see who it is, Daisy, or not?

DAISY: 'Not' sounds good to me, Ralph.

> *(Doorbell rings again.)*

RALPH: Alright, alright. I'll get it. But don't you dare light that. . . thing up.

(He crosses to door. She lights a cigarette.) #2

Discussion Questions and Exercises

1. **Art Analysis**. Take three paintings from different eras and analyze them (for the purpose of this exercise, select works that have story elements in them rather than pure abstractions). How is the action of the painting emphasized through color, mass, contrast, texture, focus, light, and shadow? Note the figures and movement within the painting, especially the use of line, eye, and light focus as well as the use of the triangle. If the figures came to life, would the subjects have directed movement toward and away from each other? In other words, the *composition* or stage picture is never totally stagnant, but is always pushing to find the next picture.

2. **Idea of Space and the Power of Asymmetry**. On Google or Pinterest look up stage designs that emphasize asymmetrical balance. Where does the energy or tension come from in these sets? How do you feel that they are appropriate for the play that they are representing? Make copies of three of these and discuss.

3. **Ground plan Questions**. Using a play that you are developing or one that you select, answer the following questions:

   • **Where?** Where is your geographical location? Have you researched the different environmental differences between, let's say, Norway, Russia or South Africa? What is the neighborhood like? What is next door or down the road? Is the feel of the place roomy, cramped, sentimental, barren, messy, smelly. . . what? Find the adjectives. What exterior light sources are there? Streetlights, neon signs, the moon, the sun, car lights? Is the neighborhood threatening, open, friendly, isolated, decaying, new, old?

   • **When?** What is the date, season, time of the day for each scene and what have you done to establish this? And ask yourself what effect these given circumstances have on the characters throughout the drama? How does your set and ground plan(s) reflect and serve these potential environmental changes?

- **What and Who?** Where, and to what extent, were your characters educated? What class do they consider themselves to be? What habits and hobbies do they have? What foods do they like? What are they in revolt against culturally, personally, or professionally? How does your environment help, reflect, or hinder communicating these aspects? What are the characters' relationships to the space they find themselves in? Are they intruders? Do they want to be there? How at ease are they? Have they been here before? Perhaps one character wants to dominate another. They might do this by taking over the favorite chair, desk, side bar of the other character. Ask yourself how they might want to use the space. Find a metaphor: are they holding court, having a contest comparable to a sporting event, involved in a seduction, or planning to undercut and belittle? How can your environment also help or play against these impulses?

- **Why?** Ask yourself why the writer chose to put these characters together in this environment at this time. What is the nature of the conflict being played out at this time and why is it being realized in this place? For example, you are directing a farce which has a wild chase in a China shop; think of the comic possibilities and the tension that can ensue.

4. **Acting Areas**. Select several pictures from Pinterest looking under "theatrical set design" and locate the different acting areas. These are areas of primary action in which climactic and social moments are realized.

5. **Prompt Book**. Select a scene from a play that you have not directed. It should have at least two characters and be an interior setting. Do the right page, left page designation described in the text, numbering your sequential blocking choices. Often it will take more than one mini ground plan to capture all the movements that you have numbered. Then do the same for an exterior scene.

Chapter 7

The Director and Auditions

MANY DIRECTORS HAVE STATED THAT casting is 90% of a successful production. Certainly, at the professional level this can be true. But casting for academic theater includes more variables such as distributing roles in terms of what the actor needs for training purposes. At any level, auditioning is a crucial area that actors need to prepare for because it is the gateway to their artistic and financial livelihood. In a sense, it is the barometer that can measure their strength in terms of their creative objectives. It is where they are most often rejected. The questions always arise as to why they were not selected. From the handshake to the final "thank you," an actor will dwell on their audition performance obsessively. As a director it is part of your job to make them feel valued, really listened to, encouraged, and that the entire experience has been a positive one. Because you are usually on a time schedule it means that you do not get into long personal conversations with the actors in terms of their backgrounds or training. That information should be in front of you on their headshots and resumes. But if you enjoyed a performance that you had previously seen them in, or if you have a common acquaintance, mentioning something along these lines tends to put the actor more at ease.

The Actor's Calling Card

At the audition, an actor will have a *headshot* with an abbreviated or one-page *resume* on the backside of the photo for you to reference. Take the time to review these before they make their audition entrance. It is not a good idea to have other actors who plan to audition there to watch someone else's audition. It should be noted that the headshot/resume is not necessarily used in all church, community, or even University theatrical endeavors, though any acting major should be required to create one for auditioning purposes.

Things to note on the headshot/resume:

- Is the photo an honest reflection of the look of the actor? In other words, is he forty but his photo makes him look 20 years old with a lot more hair?

- Has she distinguished between professional and other productions listed?

- Has she listed the name of the director after the show?

- Has he primarily played comedy or serious drama or musical comedies? Or is there a nice mix?

The abbreviated acting resume below provides all the areas that need to be covered. For a professional actor, "Broadway" and "Professional Regional" could be separate categories. I always appreciate having the director's name as well as the theater or production company where the actor has performed. Age is usually not required but an acting age range is appreciated by the director. It is also important to note any Union affiliations which could weigh heavily on the financial considerations for your production. It is also helpful to have a resume that repeats the picture on the front in a much smaller form on the back.

It is important that you are familiar with the best actor training institutions, as well as the primary professional regional theaters. Check closely into the special skills category. If you need someone who is going to use a saber in a fight sequence, it is beneficial to have someone trained in fight techniques, both armed and unarmed. You do not want a beginner doing Shakespeare, nor do you want to have to teach someone the basics of dance choreography or mime, so be sure to question the actor specifically about special abilities and experiences in these areas. At the same time, if someone is really good at juggling or just happens to know how to walk on stilts, think in terms of adding their special abilities to your directing concept. Below is an example of a resume form:

YOUR NAME

(Addresses and all phone numbers.)

Height: Union Affiliations   Eye Color:

(SAG, AFTRA, AEA, EMC, AGMA, AGVA)

Weight: Hair Color:

THEATER PROFESSIONAL *(Broadway, Off Broadway, and Regional)*:

Play:	Role:	Theater/Director:
Three Sisters	Natasha	Pittsburgh Public (dir., Joel Stein)

(They should list all roles, or indicate if they are listing the most important or relevant.)

THEATER ACADEMIC *(or other to include Community)*

The Mysteries	Noah's Wife,	Trinity Western Univ. *(dir. Lloyd Arnett)*
	Mary Magdalene	

FILM, TV, AND RADIO

ESCAPADE (w /Tony Hale) Supporting. Myriad Pictures, (*dir.* Monty Pile)

(Expect the auditionee to list the kind of role, not necessarily the character's name, Supporting roles, Principles, Extra's, Featured, Voice Over, and student projects if relevant, etc.)

EDUCATION AND TRAINING

MFA, Acting, Regent University, Virginia Beach, Va. (2019–2022)

BFA, Acting, Carnegie Mellon University, Pittsburgh, Pa. (2015–2019)

Meisner Technique, Master Class, Goodman Theater, Chicago *(Joe Chaiken)*

Stage Combat: Unarmed, fencing, quarterstaff, broad sword, rapier and dagger *(M. Kirkland)*

Vocal: Alexander Technique (*Eric Harrell*)

SPECIAL SKILLS

Singing/Dancing: Mezzo Soprano, six years of ballet

Dialects: Irish, Scottish, English, Cockney, Indian Continent, Arabic, Spanish

Instrumental: Trumpet and recorder

Movement: Mime, (*Lecoq Institute, Charles Farceur*)

Stand-up Comedy

Circus Acrobatic

The Audition

Find a suitable auditioning space (I recall auditioning in January in New York City in rooms that were not well heated, and where everyone felt the cold.) You will need to make sure that publicity includes directions on how to get to the space with phone numbers to register in large print. Arrive early and make sure the stage manager or assistant stage manager has set up what you require for the auditions. Soundproofing is important because you do not want those waiting to audition to hear those on stage or in an adjacent audition room.

Besides considering if the actor is the physical and emotional type for the role, what do you look for during this short audition process?

- Does the actor exhibit an understanding of the monologue she is performing? Too often, especially in auditioning for classical plays, actors have memorized the lines but have little idea of what they really mean. This is a red flag.

- Does the actor have any physical or verbal handicaps that would obviously impede the realization of the essence of the character? You probably will not be able to overcome these during a short rehearsal process. Another red flag.

- Does the actor repeat excessively verbal or physical patterns that seem to be more tied to the performer than the character represented?

- Does the actor rush through the audition piece? This is a sign of a beginner.

- Has the actor cluttered up the performance with inappropriate props or costume pieces?

- Does the actor stay rooted to one spot? Seeing how they can move in relation to the evolving narrative is something you want to be able to evaluate. Have him sit and take off a shoe during the audition, or give him a broom and have him sweep, or have him sit and stand again when he feels most motivated. Is he able to integrate the new movement requisites with the script in an organic way?

- And of utmost importance, is the actor able to recognize and take us through the beat transitions in the script? Hopefully there will be one or two. This means organic movement. Changes in focus, rhythm, pacing, breath, and intensity are what characterize a beat transition. It is up to you to recognize the transition in the script and ask the actor to go back to just before that moment. Briefly describe what you think is going on there, or ask her, and then tell her that she must do three things during the transition before she can pick up the dialogue. Will she find appropriate gestures and breath and movement to make the transition really sing? How imaginative are her choices? How well have they taken and understood your direction?

- Usually in a casting call, in which numerous actors are auditioning, you do not have time to work with actors in terms of possible improvisations with the script. This is primarily a function of callbacks in which there is more scheduled time with each potential performer. Here are a few suggestions about common problems: If the actor is playing one thing emotionally, perhaps he has an overriding plaintive tone and you want some variety, so give him something to play that will challenge that oneness. Find a place to laugh in the piece, any kind of laugh. Or play the scene as if he was a fast-talking used car salesman. Anything to break the pre-imposed mold and test his imagination.

Part of the directing process is having the skill and imagination to find relative images and actions to make the actor more responsive, more driven, more focused, and more imaginative. My first choice is to find an improvisation that involves some aspect of a physical action to help the actor explore more challenging possibilities in the monologue.

After the actor is finished, thank him. Let him get through his entire audition even though you might be able to tell in the first minute that he is not right or has limitations. Notify him that callbacks will be posted, etc. If you are interested in the actor, you might also check to see if he is essentially free for the rehearsal period and performance dates through the stage manager.

A side note: I usually ask the stage manager at the audition to be aware of any negative or positive behavior before the actors do their audition. While on stage during the audition an actor will be sweet and accommodating. But this could be a cover up for demanding, pushy, or negative behavior while waiting for her audition. Some examples of behavioral anomalies that I have run into are listed below under callbacks.

CallBacks

After the auditions you will publish *callbacks* for those actors who have made the first cut. Do not callback actors that you are not interested in. Callbacks often involve cold readings where actors are matched up with each other and given a bit of time to work through a scene before they work in front of the director. What are you looking for here?

- This is an opportunity to see if the actors can take direction. Some of the improvisations mentioned earlier can be utilized with the individual performer. (See Appendix 2)

- Since the actor is now working with a partner, observe how well they listen to the other character and take the time to react. Are they trying to direct their partner? Are they giving and taking appropriately as the script demands; or are they dominating the situation trying to make themselves look good?

- Ask them to go off book and to play the scene. How well have they understood the scene? How are they using their imaginations dealing with the situation or are they just trying to recapture the actual lines from the scene?

- If the actor comes up to you afterwards and says about his partner, "I couldn't get her to do anything that I suggested." Red flag. Move on.

- Find an action for the actor to play that is not mandated in the script. Mary is telling George that she wants to leave him. What if you put three or four props around the acting area, and during the scene she must pack it all into a small bag? How well does she match the words to the action?

- Callbacks are also the time to get to know the actor a bit better. Who are they when they are not doing a role? Can you find the authentic individual there, the guy who grinds his own coffee and bicycles in the park?

- We all have sympathy for the actor, for the tensions, and casting anxieties. Not being cast is not being as quite-right-for-the-role as somebody else. It is not a failure. Friendliness and genuine interest are always applicable. But do not make promises or hint at results that are not going to materialize.

Cold Readings

A few notes on your selected callback process.

- Make sure that you do not pick a scene with too much business to accomplish. Pick a scene that has conflict but try to avoid scenes with physical violence.
- Be sure to outline the parameters of the space that you want them to work in.
- If you put two chairs out there, they will end up sitting in them and talking to each other.
- Provide instructions for a re-take of the scene by conveying with your voice the emotion that displays the sense of what you want without telling the actor what to do or how to do it.
- Do not direct the scene. Remember you are looking at the talent and the choices that the actor makes, not trying to block the scene.
- Watch for the positive choices of actors taking the time to react, both before and after the line.
- Always talk to the actors in terms of objectives, what the character most desperately wants.
- If actors are entering or exiting in character watch how they tell the story of the scene through their movements.
- Watch for physical quirks in the actors: swaying in place, wandering, rubbing fingers together, the same facial or hand gesture repeated too many times.
- Have the actors effectively located the beats in the scene and are they really taking the time to make the beat transitions work?

- Try to avoid too much imposed mime work. A simple and appropriate prop can work, i.e., a towel, a picture in a frame, a bag with a shoe in it.

- You can video the scene, but do not watch the video while it is being filmed. Keep the video for later to remind you of who did what.

- If actors ask a question, answer quickly and avoid over-explaining. If they are talking too much, gently cut them off and get into the audition.

- Sometimes one actor can take over her scene partner, and start directing by making suggestions about where to move, etc. *Do not allow this.*

- Simple physical touches, if agreed upon, can be used. But take the time to make this understood.

Discussion Questions and Exercises

1. **Auditions**. With a few other actors or directors get together and have each actor memorize the first 30 seconds of a monologue of their choice and present it before the group. It could be one they have written themselves. Oftentimes, an experienced director does not need more than a few seconds to know if the actor has what he is looking for in a role. Discuss after the presentation what you noticed as a director, find something to compliment the actor on, and also note what concerns might you have?

2. **Improvisation in Auditions**. In the above exercise, what improvisations would you like to take the presenter through? Why? What are you looking for? Confidence, variety, focus, gestures/movement, vocal qualities, and appropriateness to the part are to be considered. See Appendix 2 on Improvisation for more information in this area.

Chapter 8

Mounting the Production

THERE ARE MANY APPROACHES as to how to conduct this first meeting of the cast as you sit around a table and read the entire script. Some directors insist that the actors not interpret the script, just read the lines and listen. Others opt for letting the actors explore the emotional range of their characters in this first reading. Since your interpretation of the play and roles is going to be defined in the early weeks of rehearsals, having actors launch into their own interpretation of the script can be a bit self-defeating. I usually request that the script be read with intelligence and tell the actors not to worry about the full emotional possibilities of the moments, but neither to read in a monotone. In other words, reflect the reality of the moment without over-acting.

One of the most important things to keep in mind is that each actor may have a different approach to the art of acting. Some might be steeped in Meisner or Stanislavski, others in Suzuki, Benedetti, or even Grotowski.[1] As a director, just as you should be aware of the artistic constructs of lighting and music, so should you be familiar with different approaches to actor training. Differing approaches to acting can sometimes lead to tension during the rehearsal process. In directing a professional production of *Cyrano de Bergerac* (1897), the actress playing Roxanne insisted on doing improvisational work with the classically trained actor playing Cyrano. The latter in no way wanted to waste time role playing what he considered to be a self-evident moment. I had to take a break in the rehearsal to stop and discuss what was behind her motivations and his and to work out a compromise: we decided not to improvise the language but experiment with some of the physical actions that could work in discovering the moment.

The first read through rehearsal is also the time to introduce the crew members that are on hand and get them involved. Have the designers show renderings of the set design or costume elements and discuss the image contexts of yours and the designer's preliminary work. Some directors like to have two or three reading rehearsals, especially for classical drama with heavy dialogue. I prefer to discover what is going on through action, responding better to what I see rather than what I hear.

Blocking Rehearsals

You are now ready to begin to realize the physical and emotional dynamics of the script by telling the story in the theatrical space. There are two general approaches: pre-blocking and organic blocking.

Pre-blocking is when the director has plotted out the movement dynamics of how to tell the story before rehearsals begin. He has carefully drawn arrows and recorded movement patterns in the script. For a beginning director, this means that when he starts blocking, he has every cross, exit and entrance worked out on his ground plan. The pluses are that if there is truth in his pre-rehearsal plans everything goes rather quickly. A directorial moment could sound like this, "Mary, you're shocked at what he has said. You need a moment to recoup. You cross to the sofa and sit. And Joe, when Mary sits on the right side of the couch, you cross behind it, lean on it, and try to stroke her hair. Your literal action is to comfort her in her distress. Your essential action is to begin the seduction process." The problem arises when you realize that you have begun the seduction process too early, so you are going to have to make another movement choice. This begins a domino effect, because now that you have broken the logical blocking process that you have worked out at home, everything, or at least several things, must be changed to accommodate to this one alteration.

One approach I never endorse is when the director gives the actors their blocking and they record it in their books before they get on stage. Deadly theater, as Peter Brook, former director of the Royal Shakespeare Company, describes it. I do use pre-blocking if I am doing crowd scenes or large musical numbers; and I have been known to put character labels on chess pieces to work out the movement patterns. Your rehearsal schedule has hopefully mapped out what you want to accomplish in these early blocking rehearsals, and pre-blocking can be the most efficient means of assuring that you meet your goals. You should watch for a tendency to rehearse early scenes in the play for too long, leaving less time for Act Two rehearsals. Also, do schedule blocking scenes in linear sequencing whenever possible, so that you and the actors can sense the evolving structure of the story as you work toward the final climax. This is one of the advantages of theater over film—working in sequence. But at the same time, be sensitive in scheduling so that actors are not sitting around for hours at a time to rehearse just a minor moment. In other words, be sensitive to the demands of the actor's time. Note that farcical comedy, period plays, and anything highly stylized, tend to take more rehearsal time. Also know that professional and experienced actors work a lot faster than beginners. For a professional cast, figure around four weeks, for amateurs about six. Add a week or two for musicals and even more than that for original plays, especially when working with playwrights who are re-writing scenes.

Once you feel a bit more confident and perhaps have more rehearsal time, *organic blocking* is recommended. This does not mean that you have not thought about when and where you want characters to play certain moments, but it does mean that you have a bit more flexibility in reacting to movement conditions and input as they arise during the rehearsal. *Organic* implies that you communicate the moment with the actors in such a way that they are encouraged to creatively put together the motivational relationship challenges in telling the story. I usually have a very strong picture of beat transitions in terms of what I want to happen but remain flexible in terms of how I get between these transitions. There are often several workable movement possibilities in any single blocking moment, so creating the atmosphere where you are open to exploring these becomes important to the organic approach to blocking. Your dialogue with the actress might sound something like this:

DIRECTOR: That's right. You can't believe what he's telling you. You need a moment to recoup. Where do you want to go to find that moment?

ACTRESS: Let's see, I don't think I want to leave.

DIRECTOR: Good. But also, no, the script doesn't allow that.

ACTRESS: And I still want to encourage him. The sofa. It's always been a comfort.

DIRECTOR: Good, let's see how that works.

(She moves. To ACTOR.)

She's off. What do you want to do now?

ACTOR: I want to grab her and kiss her and run into the bedroom.

DIRECTOR: But. . .?

ACTOR: But I don't want to scare her off.

DIRECTOR: So?

ACTOR: So, I'll make my way over to the sofa. Slowly. Sensitively. She's hurting.

(He does this, sitting next to her.)

ACTRESS: I don't think I'm ready for him to be so close.

ACTOR: O.K., how's this? I move up behind the sofa, and I'm there but there's still an object between us.

(He does so.)

DIRECTOR: Good. But remember, your essential action is still to seduce.

ACTOR: Right, so I'll touch her hair. That could be saying, "it's going to be alright," and I've also touched her in the process. I'm not at first base yet, but I'm on the way.

Thus, the term organic. "But Gil, what if the actress wants to go to the spindle back chair instead of the sofa, and you really want her on the sofa?" Explore it. Try it. If it does not work, you could say something like this: "the chair is cold, static, doesn't have much room to go anyplace. Let's try the same motivation but going to the sofa instead. It's been a refuge for you ever since you were a kid." This does take more time, but the process is exploratory, and often the talent will come up with choices that are competing with yours. Directing in terms of character motivation rather than in terms of rigid space requirements becomes a more creative and democratic process where everyone involved feels that they are contributing.

Communicating with the Actor

Over time, you will develop an approach to communicating with the actors that best fits your style and artistic tendencies.

I have found three approaches to be fruitful in terms of defining beats, objectives, and internal processes. The first is Literal and Essential actions as described in *A Practical Handbook for the Actor* (1986), which represent effective tools for actor/director communication. They are also defined and further explored in Chapter 5. You are encouraging the actor to be playing two things at the same time, one technical the other motivational. They take specific form during the beat transitions. They define the physical action and the internal motivation for the action of the beat and sometimes the entire scene.

As a director I am always trying to communicate to actors that they should be playing two things at any one time. If the actor is realizing both the physical action and the essential action it deepens the performance; it assures that subtext will be played; and it can heighten the tension in a scene because the two actions can also be opposed to each other. Thus, the character is crossing in to shake his father's hand to say goodbye, but he really would like to bash the old man on his head. This also has a spiritual component in that even in personal interactions with others, we are aware of our calling and discipline in attempting to be an image of our Lord, Jesus.

Actor's Objective and Inner Monologue

The actor's objective is to *want* something. But you should not stop there. The next step is to establish strategies as to how the actor is going to get what she wants in any beat. My argument is that, whenever possible, describe the action of a beat, not merely in terms of what state the actor is in or what she wants, but come up with strategies for getting what she wants in physical terms. For example: The agreed upon objective for a beat is "to get your friend Ralph out of the room as fast as possible." Then explore all the physical possibilities of doing that.

1. Edge him toward the door.
2. Hand him his coat and his hat.
3. Shake his hand and tell him, "It was nice."
4. Feign an awful headache.

Of course, the script is going to have a lot of input into these actions, but any one of the above will involve a physical commitment to the moment. You might also think in terms of a *pulling action* or a more *pushing action*. Is it possible to push or pull without grabbing on to Ralph? It is. Thinking in terms of pushing or pulling is helpful, because it focuses the action on running toward or running away, on possession or disassociation, on necessity or rejection, and does not necessarily have to be articulated as overt physical action. Language can fulfill similar functions in terms of being considered as action.

This brings up the next important factor. Set an objective that has a strong physical action, which cannot be accomplished onstage because of the script. For example, tell the actor: "You want to slap Ralph unconscious and drag him out of the room as soon as possible." The script does not allow this, but because of the desperation of this internal want, the audience will sense the tension in the character's voice, see the way she clasps her fingers into a fist, the impatience, the need, and so forth.

Perhaps the character is in a wheelchair and can only move his head. You can still create for the moment strong physical action objectives because this will then create tension in the character's voice, breath, and the face and head which could be apparent.

Another technique that I use, especially when the beat is being rushed or misunderstood, is to ask the actor to play the beat transition moment out loud, so that I can determine what she is thinking. We then talk about objectives and strategies and given circumstances based on her internal dialogue as well as the verbal script. I call this the Inner Monologue which can be:

- The character's first-person intimate reaction to what is going on.

- Prepared in the rehearsal process until it becomes second nature, and the actor/character does not need to consciously think about it.

- An excellent check to see whether the actor is in the moment.

- A way for the director and actor to communicate about the inner process of what the character is going through at any moment. It can be played in rehearsal out loud, and used effectively in an audition to assess an actor's training, specificity, and imagination. It focuses the actor on sensory tasks, given circumstances, and sequence of actions in the scene.

Let's say that Bruce is coming to Jan's apartment to break up with her after a long engagement. In rehearsal, he enters and goes right to her. You want to explore this moment in a more specific and deeper way. You ask him to perform an inner monologue, noticing and commenting on at least five aspects of the scene before he wakes her up from sleeping at her work desk. Find an action or a focus for each thought. The actor might come up with the following:

BRUCE: She's asleep. Good thing I didn't knock. Maybe I should have. Place is a mess, nothing new there. She's been smoking again. Window's open. Freezing in here. Don't close it, Bruce.

Don't change anything. This will be your last time. . . She's so beautiful...when she's asleep. You can't back out now. Should I wake her up? Wait it out? What the hell. Here goes.

The actor is playing sensory tasks, he is observing, reacting, providing the character with choices, and all of this will be reflected, hopefully, in breath, and small gestural expressions that will make the moment rich and believable even though during the actual expression of the moment he does not say anything.

For the first blocking rehearsal I try to get prop doubles for every scene in the play. These are put in a box marked with the scene number and used from day one. This includes any hand props, important character and costume props, or pieces that will affect the actor's performance. To suddenly ask an actor to use a cane halfway through the rehearsal process is presumptuous. The props, scarves, and even wigs will affect movement and characterization as well as give you blocking suggestions when utilized by the actor. They are important elements that help tell the story of the play you are directing. An added benefit is if you give an actor a prop in a scene, and they are carrying a script at the same time, they will be more motivated to learn their lines quickly to free themselves up. (See Appendix 3 on Prop Usage).

By the time rehearsals begin, I will have selected musical cues and styles that I want to use in the production concept. Having the music play before the nightly scene work begins, and even during breaks, can be an effective mood creator. Sensitive actors will respond to this auditory input. In a production of *Oh, Dad, Poor, Dad* (1963), director Charles McGaw had the entire cast playing percussive rhythms throughout the auditorium and the set to establish the movement and rhythmic feel of the Caribbean.

Remember, it is the beat transitions that are the key moments to realize meaningful visual and action elements and to work through changes in objectives. Same thing with scene transitions, especially in plays that have multiple scenes. I have been known to begin directing Shakespeare with rehearsals that move the actors through scene transitions before I start beat work on realizing the text.

Beat transitions will always involve movement of some sort. If you do not rehearse a play beat-by-beat, you run the risk of the actors not fully understanding the story motivationally and this leads to confusion on their and the audience's part.

Further Thoughts on the Rehearsal Process

- **Directing is about specifics.** You want the actor to take a long drink from the soda can. "Don't rush it, Pa. You know when you finish you're going to have to face him. You're thinking about what you're going to say and do."

- **Use your set.** Do not play just in front of it. Couches are made to sleep on, perch on, swoon on, make love on, slouch on, and so on. Frame the actor within the lines and function of the furniture and set pieces.

- **Sculpt your actors.** I often do exercises with poles in which the entire cast will have poles and move in a restricted area on stage in constant exaggerated but slow-motion movement. The trick is that you can only touch another person's pole with yours; you cannot make body contact with another person. You also must lie down, squat, stretch, and make sounds appropriate to your movement. This teaches concentration and awareness of fellow actors, and with some training encourages the actors to sculpt their physical relationships to set pieces and other actors rather than everyone just lining up. It builds awareness of mood and character in a moment on the stage through physical image constructs.

- **Always be reacting.** If actors are not speaking on stage, then they always need to be reacting.

- **Keep reminding actors of given circumstances and sensory tasks.** Actors often put these aside as they try and remember blocking and their lines. "You've just climbed seven stories. What has that done to your breath? And you're soaking wet."

- **Try to establish a context for a scene.** Ask yourself what the characters would be *doing* in this environment. Acting out an effective context is something the actor will thank you for.

- **Do not give line readings,** but in giving notes to the actor find the energy in the moment and communicate that.

- **Rehearse for process rather than results.** The results will come if you have taken the time to establish motivationally the process moment by moment.

- **Do not let actors criticize other actors.** Do not allow actors to offer suggestions pointed toward another actor's performance.

- **Develop the director's vocabulary**. You will spend a lifetime developing the vocabulary of the director. Start by not using the "I want you to cross. . ." The "I want's" become burdensome. Work more with "Let's try something else."

- **Do not over-explain**. Do not ask the actors questions which they can over-explain, because they often will, using the invitation to verbalize to avoid solving the problem. If an actor asks a question, then listen to him, because often the question implies a subtext to what the real problem is. Save the longer conversations for after the rehearsal. Wasting time in rehearsals is an offense to everyone.

- **All movement on the stage needs to be motivated**. (Example: Grandma is knitting to avoid confronting her granddaughter). Think in terms of all movement as an attempt to get to something or someone, or to get away from something or someone. The script says that Alex exits. But what he really wants is to desperately stay. His action of wanting to stay will be read in the way that he exits. Find the strongest motivation for or against the movement and run with it.

- **Build on the logic of moving**. Your motivational and movement complex during your show will often be built on the logic of moving (pulling/pushing) from one acting area to another.

- **Use the triangle whenever possible**. It is a powerful grouping principle. The person at the apex of the triangle will demand focus. Triangles can also be formed with furniture or set pieces. How the natural power and focus potential of a triangle is made and then dissolved into another triangle is a strong visual tool for motivating movement.

- **Mood and movement go hand-in-hand**. Characters each have different rhythms as well as actors. Study these and use them effectively. Oftentimes they can work against each other. The scene is a wake. Everyone is dressed in black and the mood is somber. Except for young Jack, who is running around the casket shooting it with a squirt gun. The Movement Handout (see Appendix 1) offers additional insight into types and effects of movement on stage.

- **Develop focus**. You want the audience to look at the right places and the right characters at the right time. Focus is how this is accomplished. Focus factors include movement, lighting, eye focus, gestural focus, set lines, and sound. For example: an actor standing at the downstage or upstage end of a sofa that is canted from up stage right to down stage left will have the natural lines of the furniture piece providing him with line focus. (See Appendix 4: Emphasis.)

- **Do not be shy of getting technical**: "Barb, counter when he moves past you." "Jim, turn downstage when you start to exit the scene." "We need to open up this moment, it's closed off to much of the audience." "Jane, we can't hear you. You're fading at the end of your lines. Find a way to keep the action moving through the language." "Ralph, your fussing with the umbrella all the time is taking focus away from the other characters." Actors are not always aware of sight lines. Your viewpoint and your adjustments are needed and most of the time appreciated.

- **Physical actions**. Developing and motivating physical actions are a key to constructing the visualization of the story elements on stage. Leaving actors to solve physical action or touch confrontations can be dangerous and often wastes time. These moments have to be broken down by the numbers, or from point to point. This is done for safety and for saving time. For example:

"We have to explore three things before you swing on Joe. The first is you need to grab his newspaper as he sits and reads it and ignores you. Let's do it. [Rehearse the moment] Good. The second thing is when he tries to stand to confront you over the lost newspaper, you need to sit him back down. Let's do it in slow motion. Joe begins to stand. How are you going to sit him down? [Rehearse the moment] Yes, that works. Now let's do it up to speed. And finally, he does stand, and you take a swing at him. Let's try it, but slow motion again, and don't actually hit him. . . we'll work the hit and response later."

This is no easy task. It is also up to the director, if you are not using a fight choreographer, to be trained in unarmed combat skills. Remember, it is the set up and follow through which are more important than the actual hit moment. The use of breath, verbal expression, and physical reaction to a fake punch or grab needs to be meticulously worked out for safety and desired effect. Any weapon used on stage needs a professionally trained practitioner to teach and coach the actors for consistent and safe interactions.

- If you want to emphasize a line of dialogue, first gesture (which gets the attention of the audience and other characters) and then say the line. An example: Joe stands suddenly, grabs his hat, his coat, rushes to the door and turns, "I'm leaving and don't expect me back." If you want to emphasize the movement, say the line first and then do the movement. Joe stands, saying, "I'm leaving, and I'm not coming back." He then grabs his things, rushes to the door, turns and glares at everyone, and leaves, slamming the door behind him.

- When giving notes, do not spend a lot of time trying to explain what you are talking about. Get the actors on their feet and do it. You will find the truth of a moment more in the repetition of doing it three times, than endlessly exploring verbally the various possibilities. So make sure you leave enough extra time after the on stage rehearsal so you can say, "Let's try it. . ." Always have actors take notes during rehearsal and afterwards. Remember that in doing a moment it becomes learned and retained in many more effective ways than just hearing the note verbally.

- When giving notes, if the actor has not correctly responded to a note you have given him in the previous rehearsal, do not hesitate to say, "This is the second time I've commented on your newspaper prop usage. What's the problem? Let's look at it."

- Do not load the actors down with notes. At the end of a rehearsal try and send the actors home with something to think about in terms of role development and problem solving.

Rehearsals After Blocking: Some Observations

About two-thirds through the rehearsal process you begin to realize that the actors perhaps now know more about their characters than you do. It is time to back off some and let them create. Keeping the discovery process going through these mid-term rehearsals is a challenge.

You should be concentrating now on rhythm and timing of moments and scenes. Does the show seem to plod along with little variety in tempo? Are the actors playing the ending of the play too early? You must coach them to be aware of the first-time nature of the moments. They have rehearsed seemingly over and over, and now they must bring a freshness and spontaneity to their work, re-discover the moments all over again, and reject the rote nature that numerous rehearsals can bring. One way to counter this is for the director to approach each rehearsal with new character/actor problems to solve and new ways to solve them. Improvisation can bring back this discovery process, but make sure that you are not just having fun or impressing the cast with your creativity but focusing the improvised moments on legitimate problems in the play.

You are also probably discovering where your original blocking or conception work is not accomplishing what you intended. Do not wait to tackle these problems. Be transparent with the cast about what is and what is not working as you take the time to correct it.

Actors identify with their characters in different ways and use different processes. Some will jump immediately into exploring the full range of possibilities that their characters present; others will creep up on their character, finding small moments of truth that eventually build into more significant moments. As the director, you need to know how to encourage, be patient, and comment on the varied progress and journeys that are being worked out in front of you. But if an actor's seeming lack of development of his character is holding the cast back from realizing their characters, then something must be said and done to encourage the actor to step out and make it happen.

By this time, you have been timing scenes and act run throughs. If you are finding that run throughs come in at over three hours, or seem tedious when they should be moving along, try and avoid the old saying of "faster and louder." Tighten up the beat transitions first. Address moments that are a bit rambling because they explain what is already understood, or areas where perhaps you and the actors have become a bit indulgent. If cuts need to be made, do not be averse to making them. But make them now, before technical rehearsals begin. Convince actors that the moment is coming across and does not need any elaboration. Suggest to actors that the internal pacing of their lines in terms of what their character is going through can be picked up. Look at exits and entrances, the time needed for scene transitions, and make sure that offstage costume and prop changes are done with timeliness. Add upbeat music and have the actors move to it, sensing the internal drive and rhythms therein. Do a speed run through, having the actors pick up their pacing both physically and verbally; but do not do it in such a way that the moments and clarity are lost, because you might find that what they are doing is close to what you are looking for. Side coach if things are slowing down, encouraging the actors to keep moving.

The Final Week: Technical and Dress Rehearsals

Perhaps the most frustrating time of this wonderful but stressful process is getting through the last week of rehearsals. You are launched into technical rehearsals and dress rehearsals.

As you begin to focus on the technical aspects of the production, the actors may feel abandoned, wondering if they are communicating the essence of the character. It is essential at this point to keep dialogue with them going. You need to be especially patient and sensitive to their ego needs at this point.

The *dry tech* is an off-rehearsal period for the actors. This is when all your attention is directed toward setting up the light and music cues that you have worked over with the design and tech crew in the previous weeks. Be sure that you have stand in representatives for the actors to make sure focus of lights and sound is aligned with your realization of the script. This is also the time that you give the process over to the stage manager and assistant stage manager by letting them call the show and realize scene change transitions. Costumes are yet to come. You still maintain artistic overview of suggesting and approving length and direction of cues, but it is your staff that will be running the show, not you.

Wet tech is next, which is a technical run through with actors. I suggest that if you have lots of cues that you run the show from cue to cue, rather than trying to play all the performance moments. Otherwise, there is a good chance that you will not get through all the cues in a single rehearsal. It is important here to remind the actors, who will be repeating moments tirelessly, to play the moments honestly and up to tempo so that correct timing can be realized especially for sound and lights. It is also a time when props can be brought on and off as needed. Make sure that the cast understands that this is the crew's time to make it right.

Discussion Questions and Exercises

1. **Triangles**. Using actors and furniture, create a variety of different triangles. Change the focus and relationships and notice what happens. Use furniture to be one of the triangle corners. Have actors use eye contact, and through gesture, line focus. Provide a few simple lines of dialogue for each and note how the emphasis on the lines changes when the nature of the triangle changes also. Have actors

elevated, sitting, and keep trying to create asymmetrical triangular emphasis. Add a prop to the scene and see how that also provides focus and emphasis as it is passed between actors.

2. **Explore the Set**. Using a sofa or a table with three chairs or even a settee, have a couple of actors explore all the possibilities that you can imagine in, on, and around the set piece. Use just a few lines of dialogue either from a script or made up. Note how as the picture changes the nature of the line delivery will also be affected.

3. **Focus**. In an acting area place a number of furniture pieces, or cubes which can be easily moved about. Using three actors create moments that deal with how movement creates focus, how eye contact creates focus, how gestures create focus, and how set lines create focus. Discuss and manipulate.

APPENDICES

Appendix 1

Movement Essentials for the Stage

Determining Movement: In determining movement for any play, the following questions should be asked:

- What is my ground plan? How much room is there for acting movement? What is the size and the configuration?
- Where are my acting areas?
- Do props and set pieces and furniture provide the obstacle course needed?
- Does my play conception feature movement as a storytelling device?

Remember: Travel the diagonals for effective movement patterns.
Motivations for Movement

- To express inner emotion
- To tell a story
- To visualize inter-personal relations
- To visualize beat, scene, and act transitions
- To reveal character
- To establish mood
- To provide motivation for another actor's line or move

Remember: Every move, be it business or action, must be motivated.
Strong Movements

- Move to a stronger acting area
- Rise
- Step forward
- To move out from behind furniture
- To move into contrast with others

- To move out from a group
- Short blocking movements tend to be stronger than long movements because they are usually motivated by a more immediate need

Remember: Vary the length, tempo, and rhythm of your movements. Rules made to be broken

- Toward is aggressive—away is passive
- Take the shortest path to the objective
- Permit all actors to be visible
- Create easy movement to subsequent stage pictures
- Avoid lining up in one line, equal spacing, copying another's body posture or stance

Remember: Never waste a movement

Appendix 2

Improvisation

IN THE REHEARSAL PROCESS, *improvisation* is a series of techniques that assist actors in discovering moments of truth. Improvisation can utilize props, made up dialogue, mime, and physical actions. The range of types and usages of improvisation is endless and only limited by the imagination of the director and actors.

It can be used:

- **To bring spontaneity back to a scene**. Actors memorize lines, and they memorize blocking. They rehearse the same scene innumerable times. After a while they can begin to take each other for granted, their environments for granted, and so on. Familiarity often breeds staleness. Improvisation at a key time in the rehearsal process breaks habits and provides a new awareness.

- **To stimulate the imagination of actors**. By taking the script from an actor's hand and asking him to think of his character in unfamiliar circumstances, you allow him to respond in a way not necessarily provided in the text. He must probe his character again and again to find the appropriate action and word responses. Your actor already has an idea of his character and how the character thinks and what he does in the scripted scene. Construct an environment or situation outside of the script that can cause the imagination of the actor to re-engage the character under different circumstances. The questioning of motivations and reactions outside of the script will allow him to question the motivations and reactions of the scene on which he is working.

- **To re-integrate concentration back in a moment or scene**. Improvisation forces the actor to listen and to watch with concentrated focus. Suddenly new words and movement are coming from her fellow actors. If she is to respond in character, then she is forced to become completely absorbed in what is going on around her. Her search for clues will become focused. So often actors forget to listen to either themselves or fellow actors during a familiar scene. Reactions become telegraphed. Lines are said methodically. Improvisation can bring new life to a scene through forced concentration.

- **To explore varied facets of the character's relationships to others and to an environment outside the text**. You can relate in a new fashion by exploring possible interactions outside the text; trying to communicate without words; and by trying out different choices.

- **To clarify objectives**. Stripped of the text, the actor can now try different strategies. There is no failure, every strategy is worth examining.

Remember:

- Always have a purpose for creating an improvisation.

- Do not let actors just talk; keep the words to a minimum. Always try to have your actors realize their objectives physically. Find physical relationships and moments that say as much as the spoken word.

- Be sure the actors know their objectives when they start the exercise.

- Keep the scene going even after everything seems to have died. Frustration will often drive the actors to discover new things about themselves and their characters. As a director, keep out of the scene and let the actors develop it. Stop when the scene seems to have effectively accomplished something. Then talk about it. What was helpful and what did not go anywhere? Have something positive to say.

- Have your actors begin the scene at once; do not let them stall around or rehearse it before they start. It is not a performance.

- The actor should not play the playwright, but only the character.

Examples:

- Have the actors play the scene or beat gesturally, not using signals, but finding physical actions that depict the inner and outer truth of the scene.

- Play the entire scene in gibberish, or using numbers, or sometimes singing it to each other paraphrasing the text.

- Have the actors create a scene that might have happened before the play began; or a moment that is perhaps offstage, creating the moment that is talked about. Two actors enter arguing. Play the argument, how it began and where it got to before their entrance.

- Change all the scenery around and play the scene.
- Place the actors in a different environment. Perhaps in a hospital room or a subway. Improvise the scene, making up dialogue or using actual dialogue of the scene.
- Have the actors play *against* the emotional outpouring in a scene. Find a way to laugh in a crying scene.
- Introduce several new hand props in the scene and have the actors find a way to use them.
- Have two actors touch, grip hands, etc. and play the entire scene without letting go, communicating what is happening through touch.
- The action is to humiliate Betsy. Explore three different ways of accomplishing this in the scene. Explore the objectives in new and inventive ways.

Appendix 3

Notes on the Use of Props

I DIRECTED A PLAY THAT I WROTE with Dr. Attilio Favorini entitled *Steel/City* (1976) which was about the rise and fall of the steel industry in Pittsburgh. It received both academic and professional productions in that city. It is a huge sprawling drama that goes from the Iron Industrial age in Pittsburgh through the development of different processes of steel making with a special emphasis on the lives of the workers.

It required a huge number of props, 500 to be more precise. The designer said he would never work with me again, though he did; but finding, refining, and marshaling this array of hand props was a gargantuan task. The result was a visual and action/context authentic journey into the lives and relationships of the steel laborers that lent creditability to the vastness of their work experiences.

I emphasize the use of props. I have facsimiles available from the very first blocking rehearsal. Props are important because they are ready instruments that help the director to tell the story of the drama in space, through expanding, characterizing, and manipulating that given space. They can also provide a visual context that can contribute to business and interrelationships perhaps not noted before. Finally, they motivate the actors to learn their lines. The actors will want to get off book so they can manipulate their cane or knitting needles in a selective and telling fashion. As a director, it is imperative that you also set due dates for when actors have to have their lines memorized. "Be off book for Act One by November 13." And stick to it. An actor who cannot or seemingly will not learn his lines on schedule will adversely affect the entire rehearsal process.

Props have a special power because they are selectively used in a meaningful fiction environment to help tell the story that is going on. There is almost a ritualized feel they can exude due to their potential symbolic significance. Because all art is selective, your choice of props is important; they stand out. Think in terms of your stage set being a location that is suddenly closed off from the world, which makes every prop in it have a charged reality. Take for example my production of *Hedda Gabler* (1891), in which the opening sequence had Hedda pacing in a darkened living room, smoking a cigarette. The prop of the cigarette spoke of her independence from the customs of the day, her rebellious spirit. Having the room filled with luggage and boxes, she and Tesman her husband having just returned from a honeymoon, lent an overbearing sense of claustrophobia, as if this house could never contain this woman. She opens a pair of pistols that were her father's, a male symbol of power that she is adopting. The list goes on.

So what do props do for the play and the character? They provide the actor with a means of defining social station, the character's age, and rhythm, and help in defining objectives. They also support and amplify verbal action. For example, try this: have an actor do one of their speeches with no props, and then have them do it while eating a meal. The timing, the emphasis, the meaningful pauses, and the character definition in terms of the way he eats, will markedly improve the communication of the moment.

Props become an extension of one's character; they are another visual element that offers character revelation. They also can work to create the opposite message: Charlie Chaplin drinking champagne or stealing appetizers at a high society party. Passing the prop becomes another way to telegraph relationship. How does a guy express love or hatred to someone in the way that he gives a newspaper he has been reading to the person? Explore the tactile nature of props. How does the prop reflect the nature of character and impending action? An effective exercise is passing the prop: having the actors exchange props to indicate the various relationships they might have with each other. What is the difference between throwing the newspaper down at someone's feet or gently folding it and lovingly passing it in such a way that the person receiving it has to come quite close? The passing of the prop tells the story of what is going on.

Some examples:

- Humphrey Bogart in the film *The Caine Mutiny* (1954) with his constant rolling of two metal balls in his hand. Stress and control are the message.

- Hedda Gabler's pistols emblemize her male tendency toward power and father fixation (1891).

- Ruth's drinking glass in *The Homecoming* by Harold Pinter (1965) serves as a seductive prop that breaks Lenny's resolve.

- The slaughtered pig in Shylock's trial scene of *A Merchant of Venice* (1605), a visual image of the desecration to all that he stands for.

- Stanley's raw bloody beef emphasizes the uncivilized, animal-like and even dangerous nature of his personality in *A Streetcar Named Desire* (1947).

- The skull in Christopher Marlowe's *Doctor Faustus* (c. 1592) presages his ultimate death. The skull in *Hamlet* (c. 1600) does the same. Who does Hamlet have to talk to but a dead clown and grave digger?

- A toy boat that Prospero is constructing causes an actual shipwreck when he blows on it in *The Tempest* (c. 1611). It helps to depict his powers as a sorcerer and his longing for revenge.

- The dagger in *Macbeth* (1606), serves as a symbol of guilt and haunting judgement.

The list goes on. Actors will thank you for providing them with appropriate, character-laden props. The only red flag: give an umbrella or a fan to a new actor and it can become a crutch and an ultimate distraction.

Appendix 4

Emphasis

A BASIC TENET OF DIRECTING a play effectively is getting the audience to look where you want them to look. Though they can choose, unlike film, to look anywhere on the stage, one of the skill sets of the director is to make sure that key moments are not missed, are not confusing or vague, and that the full impact of the story is well communicated visually and aurally. A few of the techniques of promoting effective emphasis are mentioned below:

- **Area of the Stage Emphasis**. Downstage center is your strongest area. Some would say that up left is the weakest (because we read from left to right). Any move into a stronger acting area will help establish emphasis.

- **The Actor's Focus**. Wherever the actors are looking, the audience will tend to look toward the same place. This is eye focus. If an actor is down center, facing the audience full on, she is to be considered in an emphatic position. Actors facing upstage, less so, unless they are the only ones facing upstage. An actor framed in an entrance or exit receives noted emphasis, the same as an actor in an elevated position.

- **Isolation of the Actor.** If an actor is isolated by light, if he moves out of a crowd and is individualized as being separate, if he is singing and isolated in a follow spot, emphasis will follow.

- **Movement:** of course, the moving actor will be watched. Take advantage of this by setting up a reaction to this primary movement by the other cast members.

- **Costume:** take the example from *The House of Bernardo Alba* (1945) in which all the daughters are dressed in black except for one, who is in black with a bright red petticoat. She is the one who will be watched, and she is the rebel.

- **Scenery Elements**: The diagonal line of a staircase, natural framing devices such as entrances and exits and arches, or the line of a sofa back, all are useful to provide emphasis.

- **Power Words**: having the actors hit the power words in a line or speech helps the audience to listen and comprehend what is transpiring on stage. This is especially true for period or verse drama. Words, interpreted correctly, are an action element of drama.

Appendix 5

Suggested Reading List

Ball, David. *Backwards & Forwards: A Technical Manual for Reading Plays*. Carbondale, Illinois: Southern University Press, 1983.

Ball, William. *A Sense of Direction: Some Observations on the Art of Directing*. Chicago: Drama Publishers/Quite Specific Media, 2003.

Barton, John. *Playing Shakespeare: An Actor's Guide*. New York: Anchor Press, 2001.

Brook, Peter. *The Empty Space*. New York: Scribner, 1995.

Bruder, Melissa, Lee Michael Cohn and Madeleine Olnek. *A Practical Handbook for the Actor*. New York: Vintage Press, 1986.

Brueggemann, Walter. *The Prophetic Imagination*. Minneapolis: Fortress, 2018.

Burke, Kenneth. *A Grammar of Motives*. Oakland: University of California Press, 1969.

Canfield, Curtis. *Craft of Play Directing*. Austin, Texas: Holt, Rinehart and Winston, 1963.

Clay, James H. and Daniel Krempel. *The Theatrical Image*. New York: McGraw Hill, 1967.

Cole, Toby and Helen Krich Chinoy. *Director's on Directing: A Source Book of the Modern Theater*. Austin, Texas: Holt Rinehart and Winston, 2013.

Egri, Lajos. *The Art of Dramatic Writing*. New York: Touchstone, 2012.

Frangione, Lucia. *Espresso*. Vancouver: Talonbooks, 2004.

Harris, Max. *Theater and Incarnation*. Grand Rapids: Erdmann's Publishing Co., 2005.

Hodge, Francis and Michael McLain. *Play Directing: Analysis, Communication, and Style*. Philadelphia: Routledge, 2009.

Kinemann, Laurie. *The Stage Management Toolkit*. Philadelphia: Routledge, 2016.

Langer, Susan. *Feeling and Form*. New York: Macmillan, 1953.

Long, Bruce. *The Problem with the Dot: A Holistic Approach to a Christians' Care and Cultivation of Global Culture through the Theatrical Ecosystem*. Eugene, Oregon: Wipf and Stock, 2021.

McKee, Robert. *Story: Substance, Structure, Style and the Principles of Screenwriting*. Los Angeles: Regan Books, 1997.

O'Connor, Flannery. *Mystery and Manners*. New York: Farrar, Straus and Giroux, 1970.

Ryken, Leland, et.al. *Dictionary of Biblical Imagery*, Downers Grove, Illinois: Inter Varsity Press, 1998.

Spolin, Viola. *Improvisation for the Theater*. New Albany, Indiana: New Albany Press, 2013.

Wolterstorff, Nicholas. *Art in Action*. Grand Rapids: Eerdman's, 1996.

Glossary

Act One climax: A plot point that pushes the protagonist irretrievably into committing to the action of the story that is precipitated by the point of attack.

Act Three climax: The final and meaningful resolution of the story's plot point progression in which the protagonist now ventures into the final battle and the final testing of his will against the forces arrayed against him.

Act Two climax: A major plot point that presents the conflict and action late in Act Two in which the protagonist comes closest to relinquishing her objective and being defeated by the antagonist.

apron: Any part of the stage that extends past the proscenium arch towards the audience or seating area.

Archetypal gestures: A label given by Michael Chekhov to describe his acting technique developed at the Moscow Art Theater with Stanislavsky in the early twentieth century. The gestures are as follows: open, close, push, pull, lift, embrace, penetrate, tear, smash, and throw.

arena stage, or theater-in-the-round: A performance area that is surrounded by audience members on all four sides.

a vista: Staging actions and scene changes that would normally be hidden from the audience.

beat: The smallest motivational building block that is used in structuring the plot of a story in terms of your character's objectives and goals.

callbacks: Invitations actors receive to meet with or perform for a casting director in consideration for an acting role after already having participated in the original audition.

central image concept: A pervasive image, with its organic roots in the playscript, around which the director frames or shapes his production concept.

character arc: The formation of what the characters experience in terms of physical, emotional, ethical, spiritual, and conscious-awareness change during the story's evolution.

character flaw: A negative behavior or trait that the protagonist has at the beginning of the play's problem but hopefully learns to conquer or adapt to by the end of the dramatic action.

composition: The arrangement of actors and scenery on a stage so as to create a desired effect.

Creative Mandate: God's call on us to realize creatively what it means to be made in his image.

crisis moment: A situation that motivates the central character in a meaningful and usually desperate way toward an inevitable action.

denouement: The final section of a play happening after the Act Three climax in which the various threads of the plot are drawn together and relational and thematic matters are resolved.

down stage: The front of the stage or part closest to the audience.

dry tech: The technical rehearsal that does not include any actors, only the director, stage manager, and technical and stage crews.

essential action: The internal motivation of why the character is doing the literal actions they are performing in every beat.

gestus: A Brechtian technique, is a clear character gesture or movement used by the actor that captures a moment or attitude rather than delving into emotion.

given circumstances: the who, where, what, and when environmental, historical, and situational conditions characters find themselves in while performing a play.

ground plan: An aerial perspective of the stage drawn to scale that outlines the performance space, elevations, and basic set pieces that the actors and technicians will interact with.

headshot/resume: An 8x10 close-up photograph of an actor, on the back of which is their acting resume that contains details about training and experience.

imagery: Found in the use of descriptive language that appeals to the five senses, and also in movement, lighting, prop, and color motifs that establish mood and meaning.

inciting incident/point of attack: The scene where the action that defines the premise first coalesces. It is the beginning of the point of no return for the protagonist, in which he is confronted with a problem and must take action.

improvisation: This is any unscripted dramatic performance or rehearsal tool that an actor uses to explore strategies of characters' goals and given circumstances.

literal action: What the character is doing physically in every beat.

mid-point crisis: A major plot point occurring just before the intermission break in the middle of Act Two that moves the protagonist closer to (or farther from) their goal.

mise en scene: The consciously designed arrangement of scenery and properties on stage in a play.

moral/ethical change: A process of awareness that the major characters go through in a drama that is determined through the execution and understanding of their moral or immoral actions.

organic blocking: Blocking that occurs in rehearsal when the director and actors come together on the first rehearsal and work together through experimentation and collaboration in blocking a playscript.

plot points: The milestone events, reversals, changes, conflicts, and resolutions that provide meaningful shape and direction to the dramatic story.

pre-blocking: Blocking notes for actors recorded in a script by a director before he begins rehearsals.

prompt book: The document used by the stage manager in theater both to record the director's blocking in the play text and to cue the actors and technicians during a performance.

proscenium stage: The architectural structure at the front of the stage that frames the action of the play. It is commonly a rectangular frame, and the stage curtain is directly behind it.

pulling/pushing action: Two of the five archetypal motions for the actor in physical action approaches to actor training, the other three being lifting, throwing, and tearing apart.

thrust stage: A performance area that extends into the auditorium so that the audience is seated around three sides.

upstage: The performance area or part of the stage farthest from the audience.

vomitorium: Tunnel like passages extending to a theater stage, especially a thrust stage or the stage of an arena theater, through which actors and audience members are allowed to enter and exit.

wet tech: The technical rehearsals that include full acting company and technical staff during the cue to cue before dress rehearsals.

Notes

Introduction

[1] Lenora Inez Brown, "The Real World," *American Theater Magazine*, TCG (November 2002): 82–83.

[2] Walter Bruggeman, *The Prophetic Imagination* (Minneapolis: Fortress Press, 2018), ix–xxi.

Chapter 1: Leadership and Directing Principles from the Book of Luke

[1] Archetypal gestures were labeled by Michael Chekhov in his approach to an acting technique developed at the Moscow Art Theater with Stanislavsky in the early twentieth century. The gestures are as follows: open, close, push, pull, lift, embrace, penetrate, tear, smash, and throw.

[2] Frank Burch Brown, *Good Taste, Bad Taste, and Christian Taste: Aesthetics in Religious Life* (New York: Oxford University Press. 2011), 120.

[3] Gillette Elvgren, *The Canterbury Tales: An Adaptation of Chaucer's Tales* (Virginia Beach: Blue Moon Publishing, 2018), 77–78.

[4] Susanne K. Langer, *Feeling and Form: A Theory of Art* (New York: Charles Scribner Sons, 1953).

Chapter 2: Theatrical Conventions

[1] Lucia Frangione, *Espresso* (Vancouver: Talonbooks, 2004), 96.

[2] Flannery O'Connor, "The Nature and Aim of Fiction," *Mystery and Manners: Occasional Prose*, eds. Sally and Robert Fitzgerald (New York: Farrar, Straus, and Giroux, 1969), 72.

Chapter 3: Imagery

[1] Andre Bazin, "The Ontology of the Photographic Image," *What is Cinema*, vol. 1, ed. and trans. Hugh Grey, 4th ed. (Berkeley: University of California Press, 1967), 9–16.

[2] Kenneth Burke, *The Philosophy of Literary Form*, 3rd ed. (Baton Rouge, University of Louisiana Press, 1941; Berkeley: University of California Press, 1973), 20. Citations refer to the Berkeley edition.

[3] Burke, 96.

[4] *Dictionary of Biblical Imagery*, eds. Leland Ryken, James C. Wilhoit, and Tremper Longman III (Westmont, Illinois: InterVarsity Press, 1998).

Chapter 5: Script Analysis

[1] William Ball, *A Sense of Direction: Some Observations on the Art of Directing* (Chicago: Drama Publishers/Quite Specific Media, 2003), 93–96.

[2] Melissa Bruder, Lee Michael Cohn, Madeleine Olnek, Nathaniel Pollack, Robert Previto, and Scott Zigler. *A Practical Handbook for the Actor* (New York: Vintage, 1986), 42–47.

[3] Syd Field has become known as the guru of screenwriting and published his teachings in a variety of books including *Screenplay: The Foundation of Screenwriting* (New York: Delta, 2005), *The Screenwriter's Problem Solver: How to Recognize, Identify, and Define Screenwriting Problems* (New York: Delta, 1998), and *Selling a Screenplay: The Screenwriter's Guide to Hollywood* (New York: Delta, 1989).

Chapter 6: Preparatory Work After Script Analysis

[1] Kenneth Burke, *A Grammar of Motives* (New York: Prentice Hall, 1945), 3–15.

[2] Sergei Eisensten, *Film Form and The Film Sense*, ed. and trans. by Jay Leyda (New York: Meridian Books, 1957).

[3] George II, Duke of Saxe-Meiningen, in *Directors on Directing: A Source Book on the Modern Theater*, ed. by Toby Cole and Helen Krich Chinoy (London: Bobbs-Merrill, 1963).

[4] William Ball, *A Sense of Direction*; Lagos Egris, *The Art of Dramatic Writing: Its Basis in the Creative Interpretation of Human Motives* (New York: Simon & Schuster, 1946).

Chapter 8: Mounting the Production

[1] Sanford Meisner taught his acting technique for over 65 years at the Neighborhood Playhouse in New York City and at the Sanford Meisner Center in Los Angeles and published his technique in *Sanford Meisner on Acting* with Dennis Longwell (New York: Vintage, 1987); Constantin Stanislavski is a Russian actor now famous for developing his acting system in the Moscow Art Theater and published his technique in a series of books titled *An Actor Prepares*, trans. Elizabeth Reynolds Hapgood (1936; New York: Routledge, 1989), *Building a Character*, trans. Elizabeth Reynolds Hapgood (1949; New York: Routledge, 1987), *Creating a Role*, trans. Elizabeth Reynolds Hapgood (1961; New York: Routledge, 1987); the Tadashi Suzuki method, which originated in the Japanese theater, applies a rigorous physical discipline to acting training to help the actor expand their emotional and physical power and commitment; American acting teacher Robert Benedetti has published his approach in a variety of books including *The Actor in You: Twelve Simple Steps to Understanding the Art of Acting*, 7th ed. (Long Grove, IL: Waveland, 2022), *The Actor at Work*, 10th ed. (Boston: Allyn & Bacon, 2008), and *Action!: Professional Acting for Film & Television* (London: Pearson, 2000); Jerzy Grotowski, a Polish theater practitioner, developed an experimental approach to acting that relied solely on the actor's bodies to tell the story and removed what he sees as unnecessary costumes, props, and set pieces.

Index

www.ingramcontent.com/pod-product-compliance
Lightning Source LLC
Chambersburg PA
CBHW031530120626

46545CB00005B/2078